# THE PUBLISHING GAME

ANTHONY BLOND

# THE PUBLISHING GAME

JONATHAN CAPE
THIRTY BEDFORD SQUARE LONDON

FIRST PUBLISHED 1971
© 1971 BY ANTHONY BLOND

JONATHAN CAPE LTD, 30 BEDFORD SQUARE, LONDON WCI

ISBN 0 224 00561 8

PRINTED AND BOUND IN GREAT BRITAIN
BY BUTLER & TANNER LTD, LONDON AND FROME
PAPER MADE BY JOHN DICKINSON AND CO. LTD

# CONTENTS

To David Susman, Esq., of Cape Town

'A publisher who writes is like a cow in a milk bar.'

*Arthur Koestler*

# AUTHOR'S NOTE

This confection has been laboriously put together over nearly three years against a changing background in publishing and would never have emerged without the diligence of Mrs Jacqueline Löos, who typed and re-typed the manuscript, or the encouragement of my colleague, Mr Desmond Briggs.

The author has drawn on the expertise of many in his profession and would like to thank particularly Mr James Kenyon for his help in the educational chapter; Messrs Abner Stein and Alan Rinzler for their help regarding the American situation; Mr Frank Rudman, Mr Fred Nolan and Mr Alan Earney for their guidance over the paperback chapter; Mr Alex Hamilton ('Pooter' of The Times); Mr Michael Holroyd for permissions; Mr F. H. C. Tatham (Editor of *Whitaker's Almanack*) for the Index; Mr Barry Rowland, who found errors and omissions in the MS, and Mr Michael Turner, who found more in the proofs; Mr Tom Maschler for his insistence, and Miss Gemma Fenton for her determination and patience. The last two are both of Jonathan Cape, who said – and it is still true – 'There is only one thing to remember about publishing: books about Latin America never sell, books about Nelson always do.'

A.B.

# 1

---

## The Simple Act of Becoming a Publisher

The emergent publisher needs no qualifications. He need have no degrees, no licence, no money or connections. Of the eight significant publishers to set up in England since the war, six were refugees and one was an orphan (and at least three went bankrupt). By 'publisher' I mean the entrepreneur, the owner, the big vegetable as the French say, and not anyone in his employ. Should he engage someone with publishing qualities, which consist of a delight in print, seeing in a book a vehicle for vicarious self-expression, and some self-confidence, topped with more than a dash of ego, that person will soon quarrel with him and set up on his own, or become editorial director of an established firm.

It is difficult to pigeonhole the publisher: he will care more about his product than an advertising copywriter; be too much of a gambler to become a successful merchant banker; too full of blind spots and optimism to be a lawyer; and his essential – if unreal – sense of his own importance would preclude diplomacy as a career. He will be part impresario, part missionary. He will not himself create like a composer, a painter or a choreographer, and if he writes at all he may make an unsuitable spectacle of himself, 'like a cow in a milk bar', as Arthur Koestler said.

A good 'general' publisher will care passionately for writers – more than for 'letters' – and will introduce new people to the public as frequently as is consistent with remaining solvent. Many times a year he will produce a book which he *knows* will lose him money. If he doesn't do this, he forfeits his own self-respect and the esteem of the professional literati, who expect the occasional obvious sacrifice.

Publishing is above all a business that depends on a constant stream of ideas. Ideas for books do not come to publishers when sitting at their desks – in which position they are least constructively employed. Some publishers may smell them on the wind, others through the fumes of too much hock over lunch. They may be prompted by the currency of a new expression like 'The Establishment', by a newspaper cutting about a hermit, or by a genuine desire to reform – the unions, the church, the civil service, the police force, the condition of the seal population, the British obsession with pets or the American with money. A publisher need not be a polymath but he must be interested in anything, and his ideas, good, bad or indifferent, must jump out of the top of his head to be bounced around by his colleagues at least once a week, or his list will falter.

Above all, a publisher must circulate. It doesn't particularly matter where, so long as it is in circles appropriate to his taste where literacy generally obtains. This may involve drinking wine by the glass in a Bloomsbury pub, using an international social position to attract authors (and vice versa), or lurking in the obscurer embassies of Eastern Europe off Belgrave Square. Not only the chairman or managing director are responsible here, of course; one wouldn't expect to find the Right Hon. Harold Macmillan propping up the bar at the Dog and Duck in Soho as he digests his third *vieux ceps* of the evening. But if there is not one member of his august house cognizant with at least the fringes of bohemia, the Macmillan novel list would begin to lose verve.

There are two broad categories in publishing: general, or trade as they say in America, which covers novels, biographies, children's books, anything in fact to interest homo sapiens; and educational, which runs from the simplest ABC to the most turgid exposition of the latest development in metallurgy. Naturally, most successful firms have many kinds of book in their lists; a publisher who set out to produce only contemporary poetry would not stay in business long without assistance from the Arts

Council, the C.I.A. or the long purse of a wealthy wife.

Great publishing houses in England and America started from oddly assorted beginnings. Cassell's,* for example, were originally the printers of tracts which were wrapped round small parcels of tea. John Murray,† by way of contrast, was in its early days the publisher of Byron and Disraeli (though Disraeli later moved to Longman's,‡ and describes with giddy pleasure how in 1870, when he was out of office, Mr Longman paid him ten thousand pounds for *Lothair*).

The mass literacy of late-Victorian England spawned a number of publishers, ranging from specialists in Penny Dreadfuls to publishers of inspirational books. (Mr Pontifex, Samuel Butler's prototype for Victorian hypocrisy, sadism and success in *The Way of All Flesh*, was a publisher.) The next publishing revolution – that of paperbacks – swept forward on the back of the mass demand for information, pleasure and titillation. The paperback business has become so successful that it is dignified on the stock exchange and in Wall Street with the title 'industry', and it threatens to overtake its aged carriage-borne parent, the hardback publishing house. As we shall see in Chapter 6 when we study a publisher's balance sheet, paperback revenue is the main source of profit to a modern hardback publisher of adult fiction.

Hundreds of publishers are listed in *The Writers' and Artists' Year Book* in England, and *Literary Market Place* in the United States, but only a fraction of them are interesting or require explanation. Anyone could tell what the business is of the Society for the Propagation of Christian Knowledge. Appendix II will provide a list of the characteristics and size of a selection of London publishers to give the bare bones of the business; now let us consider the flesh.

---

* Bought by the American firm of Crowell-Collier Macmillan in 1969 for two million pounds.
† Still eponymously owned and independent.
‡ As of 1971, part of the Cowdray organization.

## Three Brief Lives

In the opposite seat in the Brighton Belle is a man in his late thirties; black coat, striped pants, bushy eyebrows, the flared nostrils of an orator, dark hair greying at the Temples, Inner probably – right! A barrister. It is less easy to detect a publisher. Tom Maschler of Jonathan Cape, the publisher of this book, could be a conductor or a film director; Sir Rupert Hart-Davis looks like a country member; Clive Allison of newly minted Allison and Busby looks younger than most schoolboys. We have chosen first the oldest, secondly the biggest and thirdly one of the most adventurous firms, exemplified by an administrator with a passion for learning, a patrician who is passionate for animals and Africa, and a man passionate for his imprint.

### John ('Bruno') Brown of Oxford University Press

The oldest and grandest imprint in the world is that of Oxford University Press, publishers of good books since the fifteenth century. Its first jab in the arm was delivered by the unlikeable ('the reason why I cannot tell ...') Dr Fell, who moved the Press into the Bible and prayerbook business. The second was the gift of the copyright in Lord Clarendon's *History of the Great Rebellion* – hence the Clarendon Press, which still within the O.U.P. produces books of profound scholarship. The third was the achievement of *The Oxford English Dictionary*, begun in 1884 and ended in 1928. In terms of output by title and employees, the Oxford University Press is the most considerable in England. It employs 2,500 people, publishes some 900 titles a year, of which 750 come from university confrères in other parts of the world, and keeps about 16,000 titles in print.* The Oxford University Press has a jargon, set-up and purposes all its own. Working under the Secretary to the Delegates of the University Press are five figures with the Kafkaesque titles of the 'Controller', the 'Printer', the 'Secretary', the 'Publisher' and, for the Oxford University Press Inc. in the U.S.A., simply the 'President'.

* The average invoice value of an O.U.P. book is 51p, and 60 per cent of their titles sell less than six copies a month.

The 'Publisher' – the man whose name appears upon the title page – has, since 1956, been Mr John ('Bruno') Brown. After enjoying, which Evelyn Waugh evidently did not, an education at Lancing, he went to Hertford College and joined the Press in 1937 aged twenty-one. Mr Brown had neither money for a partnership, nor relatives in the business, and without these pre-requisites a career in publishing was as inaccessible then as it is today. But he did have a science degree, thought then as now to be of value in unrelated fields, and he was whipped off to India by O.U.P., with whom he has stayed ever since. From the marble halls of the Bishop of Ely's former London palace, Mr Brown publishes, in one way and another, a lot of information; but he will tell very little about the Press (his time as a Japanese p.o.w. did not melt a natural reticence). O.U.P.'s turnover must be between three and five million pounds, but since it has no share-holders, no outside money and contributes nothing to the univer-sity, its profits are not known.* It has its own paper mill (run by the 'Controller'), its own very special Oxford India Paper, and prints a third of its own books. About 73 per cent of its business is overseas and is conducted from branches all over the world, including an office with a staff of sixteen in Tokyo. (N.B. The Inter-Firm Comparison, to which publishers may subscribe to learn how they are doing in comparison with their colleagues, maintains that net profits rise in direct proportion to export turn-over.) Mr Brown, as yet only a C.B.E., conveys the solidarity and sense of purpose of the best kind of Permanent Secretary and maintains that the function of the O.U.P. is, to quote the man who founded Yale University Press at the turn of the century, 'a mission fairly described as university extension work of the finest kind'. 'We in the Oxford University Press', he says, 'have a phrase which we keep constantly in mind: "books which will advance scholarship, education and *religion*".' (My italics.)

There is no collection of T'ang poems so remote, no calculus

* Since Professor Sir Humphrey Waldock delivered his report to the O.U.P. they have disclosed some figures. Bound books out of O.U.P., U.K., add up to over £6 million per annum and, for the rest of the world, one can add another 50 per cent. This figure excludes print and paper.

so advanced, no theory of epistemology so confusing that it cannot be or has not been put out as a book by the Oxford University Press – and, ironically, it (eventually) sells. Then there are the Bibles, six hundred different bindings worth of Bibles. The Oxford University Press, less inhibited than its commercial colleagues by worries about a 'cash-flow', does not blanch at an investment of fifty thousand pounds in a work, and allows its editors great freedom;* hence their first publication of the then unknown Christopher Fry, their racily illustrated edition of the Old Testament and their sumptuous children's books. Mr Brown is, he claims, careful not to exploit the Press's relative financial immunity to undercut commercial publishers, and complains only when O.U.P. publishes at great expense a scholarly work by a bright young don, making his name for him and establishing a demand for his work, only for a commercial publisher to snap up his more saleable and popular books: 'This is a situation which is hard to bear.' Philip Guedalla, famous for his biographies and pyrotechnical style, was published by Hodder & Stoughton, but his first work, an academic study of eighteenth-century diplomacy, was issued by O.U.P.†

### Billy Collins of William Collins, Sons & Co.

When at the age of thirty Collins came south from Glasgow, where for a hundred years the family print factory had been punching out Bibles and prayerbooks under licence from the Scottish Bible Board, he found that the general publishing side of the family business had few names beyond Michael Arlen, Rose Macaulay and Agatha Christie. Now, William Collins, Sons & Co. is the biggest commercial publisher in London, a public company (with a turnover of ten million pounds) of which 40 per cent is held by his family. Although inside the 'house' it is stressed that nepotism is not the basis for promotion (the managing director, though a Scot, is no relation), Sir William can look round at his brother Ian, his son Mark, his son-in-law Philip Ziegler, and two

* Even to the extent of allowing a jacket face to bear no title, viz. Richard Lannoy's *The Speaking Tree.*
† *The Partition of Europe* (1914).

other young Collinses in their twenties, and reflect that he is something of a patriarch. His wife Priscilla is the director of religious books, and it was her interest in literature which gave Billy, self-confessedly no scholar, his interest in general fiction and non-fiction, as opposed to the Bibles, dictionaries, cheap children's books and even, at one time, lavatory paper with which the firm of Collins was identified.

Dynamic, restless, inspiring and exacting loyalty, absorbed in detail and just plain lucky, Billy Collins has all the qualities of a successful divisional commander. The promotion by Messrs Collins of such best-sellers as *The Wooden Horse* by Eric Williams, *Struggle for Europe* by Chester Wilmot, the Alanbrooke and Montgomery memoirs, *Moulin Rouge* and all the *œuvres* of Alistair MacLean is recollected with awe by the bookselling trade and with distaste and envy by his more refined colleagues. Booksellers throughout the world were almost battered into accepting piles of Collins books, attending receptions and co-operating in the steamroller process initiated by the late Sidney Goldsack and Ronald Pollitzer, two of Billy Collins's most powerful employees.

And then the luck ... Joy Adamson, padding around London from publisher to publisher, rejected* and penniless, stopped by the offices of the Harvill Press (owned by Collins) and said to Marjorie Villiers that she was dying for a cup of tea. The photographs in her hand were of the now internationally known star performer, Elsa the lioness. Marjorie Villiers telephoned Billy Collins, who pounced, and the result is well known.

Whatever acumen brought Boris Pasternak's *Doctor Zhivago* through the Harvill Press to Collins, it was luck that a storm arose about the author's acceptance of the Nobel Prize. At about the same time, Eisenhower appeared to denounce his former colleague, Field-Marshal Montgomery, whose memoirs also appeared *chez* Collins. It was in this month that the firm turned over – in all areas, admittedly, but what a sum – one million pounds.

* She had indeed been rejected by the *firm* of William Collins, Sons & Co.

Collins, though a huge firm, is a conventional British publishing outfit: they own Hatchards and used to own Better Books;* they do a mere £400,000 in school textbooks, and their Old Etonian editors point a little ruefully to the fourteen first novels which they published in spring 1969, to the exquisite natural history library and to their little guides to foreign countries, which at 40p are probably the best value in the business. But Collins are blessed, or damned, with the reputation for being the biggest promoters of blockbusters in the U.K. and overseas. If the man in the driver's seat (who also lives in the building) should ever have to get out, it is difficult to see who could hold the quadriga together.

## André Deutsch

J. H. Fabre, describing the cigal's life cycle, most of which is spent underground, begs his readers not to complain at the noise this little beast creates when he breaks through the sullen earth to celebrate life in the open air.

Could one reason for the Jewish pre-eminence in the 'business' of the arts be the fact that they were bottled up in ghettos for two thousand years, restricted to professions as embarrassing as peddling and usury, emotionally locked in the practice of an intense religion? Released during the nineteenth century on to the very open markets of Europe and America, Jews quickly established positions as impresarios in the arts. Diaghilev, Reinhardt, Duveen and Mike Todd were of Jewish and, in the case of Mike Todd, rabbinical parentage. Many publishers on both sides of the Atlantic and in Europe are of Jewish origin: in America, Mr Alfred Knopf of that Inc., Henry Simon of Simon & Schuster, and Kurt Enoch, the founder of The New American Library and, in Germany, of Tauchnitz Books; in England, the original Heinemann, the still original Mr Fredric Warburg, Sir Victor Gollancz, Mr Michael Joseph, the Franklins who owned Routledge & Kegan Paul, the Hon. A. G. Samuel who owns most of Barrie and Rockcliff, Sir

---

* Sold in 1970 to John Calder. Better Books is an instance of a bookshop's identity persisting despite the management. It was started by Tony Godwin, a controversial, no longer frightfully young, whizz-kid, who then became editor of Penguin Books, had a row with Sir Allen Lane, and is now George Weidenfeld's highly paid chief editor.

George Weidenfeld, Mr Paul Hamlyn and Mr Ernest Hecht who owns the consistently profitable Souvenir Press, to name but a few. There must be something about the revised, emancipated Jewish temperament which draws so many of that race into the world of the impresario. And what is a publisher – at best an inspirer, developer, and exploiter of talent – but an impresario?

André Deutsch was born in Hungary and came to England in 1939. At the age of twenty, on the outbreak of war, he was interned on the Isle of Man, and there met a cousin of Arthur Koestler with a small, mildly pornographic business as a publisher. Released from the camp, he was turned down by the R.A.F. and rejected as a potential Bevin boy, where he might have met another refugee, Paul Hamlyn. André's first job was with Nicholson & Watson, a firm which had been resurrected after going bust over Lloyd George's Memoirs. The Watson family – Graham Watson, one of the family, is the head of the literary agents Curtis Brown (see Appendix III) – made enough money from the manufacture of Skipper's brisling to finance an incursion into publishing. Young Deutsch was soon making enough in salary – £2,500 a year, a lot in those days – to save, and although he did a full day's work at Nicholson & Watson he invented Allan Wingate, Publishers, in a few rooms in Cumberland Place just at the end of the war.* His first success, by Maclaren Ross, was called *Bitten by a Tarantula*, and he well remembers an order from Boots (now barely in the book business) for a thousand copies. He was soon successful enough to plunge wholly into his own enterprise and has stayed, with various ups and downs, an independent publisher of general books ever since. Allan Wingate's early hits after *Bitten by a Tarantula* were *The Naked and the Dead* by Norman Mailer, *How To Be an Alien* by George Mikes (a fellow Hungarian) and *Operation Cicero* by Elyesa Bazna. Boardroom quarrels forced him to leave Wingate in 1952

* The author was employed at Allan Wingate at the time when their amiable proprietor, Mr Anthony Gibbs, decided to go into voluntary liquidation just as they were publishing the best-seller *Exodus* by Leon Uris. 'Mr Wingate' was invoked in that office when creditors became oppressive, and it was said that he only signed cheques on Friday. He did not of course exist.

and he started his own firm, achieving early success with the Memoirs of von Papen, the illicit employer of *Operation Cicero*'s author. Serial rights were bought by the late Sam Campbell of *The People* for thirty thousand pounds, and André Deutsch was clearly on his way.

The capital of André Deutsch Ltd is still an original £7,000 and his achievement with a current turnover of £500,000, plus a reputed rights revenue of about £40,000, puts André in the rare position of being an independent publisher* at the top of the Second Eleven. The kind of titles which appear under the André Deutsch imprint are of the newsworthy, possibly flash-in-the-pan variety. Names like Cohn-Bendit and Hochhuth (of *The Soldiers*) are characteristic of his list, but he has also published some distinguished fiction; witness the presence of V. S. Naipaul and Jean Rhys. Such a list can only be acquired and kept up by a succession of fast moves, a lot of hard work, opportunism and quick talking.

At twenty past six on a Friday evening in winter, André is at his overloaded desk, surrounded by telephonic equipment but preferring as an instrument of communication the human voice, raised sharply. A secretary enters and is told with a delicate smile, 'I cannot say "kind regards" to a Prime Minister whom I don't *know!*' The letter has to be retyped. Nervy, charming and disarming, vigilant in his affections but never forgetting a slight, André Deutsch is not the easiest of men to work for. Sales managers come and go as frequently as French foreign ministers before the war; letters go on being retyped long into the night; colleagues are summoned for Saturday morning summit conferences; and exacting cables arrive from Ankara – André spends at least four months of the year whizzing round the world. In her elegant autobiography, Diana Athill, a doting colleague, describes André as needing only a fast car, a bright shirt and enough money to give dinner to a pretty woman. Privately modest, André is only passionate for his imprint. You could say that André Deutsch was in love with André Deutsch Limited.

---

* As independent as it is possible to be with Time-Life holding a 40 per cent stake. Time-Life owns Little, Brown in Boston, from whom André had the Khrushchev Memoirs, 40 per cent of Rowohlt in Germany and 60 per cent of Laffont in Paris.

# 2

---

## Authors

No publisher is buried in Westminster Abbey or lolls in stone draperies among the Immortals at the Panthéon, but the fame of writers can endure for ever. A publisher may leave his dent on the literary scene during his lifetime, but when he dies the cutting edge of his imprint goes with him. Then his firm is bought over by a group or, more rarely, turned into a vehicle for the self-expression of a younger editor.

Publishers should regard authors, who are the source of their bread and butter, cake and occasionally caviare, with humility, respect and affection. A literary agent may choose a publisher for his client because of the reputation a house has for aggressive salesmanship, generous advertising, prompt payment and lucid royalty statements, an ability to exact a high advance from paperback publishers, or simply because they lunched recently.

A writer's reasons for going to one publisher rather than another are more blurred and more haphazard. He may be attracted by the other authors on the publisher's list, or he may, like Lytton Strachey, have listened to the advice of a friend.

The following account of an author's relationship with his publisher has not dated, although the events it describes took place fifty years ago. I am indebted for it to Lytton Strachey's most recent biographer, Michael Holroyd (who has received a fee for permission for this extract to be published),* and the story

---

* This is said without rancour; Mr Holroyd fights furiously for his profession, e.g. the Public Lending Right issue.

is quite simple. Lytton was looking for a publisher. *Landmarks in French Literature* had been commissioned by Hutchinson and its success led to Lytton wooing and being wooed in publishing circles. On Clive Bell's advice he sent the manuscript of *Eminent Victorians* to Chatto & Windus. The publisher's 'readers' were enthusiastic, and Chatto & Windus sent a contract offering Strachey 15 per cent on the first 1,000 copies and 20 per cent thereafter (by today's standards a staggering royalty for a first book).

The book emerged unsung on May 9th, 1918, and the publisher forgot to send the fifty pounds advance for weeks and weeks. Finally, when it looked likely that there would be a reprint, Strachey brought up the little matter and received a cheque with their apologies.

Let's take it from there:

After this false start, the relationship between Strachey and Chatto and Windus grew to be extraordinarily cordial. They are always seeking out ways and means to pay him extra money (without any prompting from Strachey), always improving the mouth-watering clauses in his contracts and subsequently breaking them for his increased benefit. They press him not to hurry with his next book; they offer to grapple with the tax authorities on his behalf; they send him innumerable dust jackets and alternative bindings from which he is asked to select his favourite; then out of the blue they write to congratulate him, in general terms, on nothing in particular, and urge him, for his own protection, to submit all negotiations to the Society of Authors. They even arrange for him to witness the printing of his books, though the moment he appeared all the machinery broke down and came to a halt, much to their confusion – and probably to Strachey's relief.

And Strachey, too, is the last word in courtesy. He invariably makes pressing enquiries after the health of the partners (even the retired ones), apologises for the slightest delay and for the legitimate correction to proof copies, recommends a friend of his to join the firm, will not listen to offers from other publishers. Perhaps best-selling authors still enjoy relationships such as this. But for the rest of us it is something to savour in all its charm, and to marvel at long and deeply.

There is still no reason why an author shouldn't stay married to one publishing house for the whole of his writing life, but we live in an age of divorce and removals. Further, in the fifty years since *Eminent Victorians* the publisher has taken a diminishing share of an increasing market in communications. In other words, whereas in Strachey's day the revenue from a writer came mostly from journals and publishers, the successful young writer of today will depend far more on television and film work. Bright British novelists like Simon Raven, the late James Kennaway, Frederic Raphael, Margaret Forster, both the Drabbles and Melvyn Bragg, not to speak of Len Deighton, can make a thousand pounds or more for a television play, and between five thousand and a hundred thousand dollars for a screenplay, which renders them less attentive to the demands of their publishers. However, the emergent author still needs a publisher to help him tenderly out into a glary world.

Authors work alone (unfashionable, in the twentieth century), and they are prone to all the neuroses of lonely* people. Few have the placidity, modesty, competence and industry of Anthony Trollope. Many are shy or aggressive, others are naive, touchy or touching; some combine all these qualities. Like vintage cars and indoor plants, authors must be treated with love and care if they are to be kept. When an author leaves a publisher or is led away by an agent, the cry is that he or she was not 'loved' enough. This means that the publisher did not watch his/her play on television last Tuesday; was not sympathetic about his/her divorce; will not reprint his/her last novel although it sold

---

* Most authors have little contact with their public. B. S. Johnson received eight letters for eight books published, most of them abusive.

out; is devoting too much attention to a new, shiny young author. A conscientious publisher may find himself becoming a nanny, banker, doctor and travel agent to an author. This might mean the loan of 'only' a fiver and a pair of socks in the middle of the night; hospitalizing for 'only a few days' an aged and incontinent red setter;* or explaining to some shy violet that publishers don't control who appears on the Frost Programme.

This sort of attention is half of the author/publisher relationship and a publisher can only duck his duty by developing some ingenious neurosis of his own. One author was dismissed from a publisher's office on the grounds that he had made a secretary cry. He withdrew angrily to a rival house, where the agent procured a larger advance. But nine months later he repaid the money and came crawling happily back to be welcomed as only a prodigal can be. He had been well edited by the other publisher but (he explained) there hadn't been enough *rows*.

Like good cooks, authors need criticism. Before the war, Messrs Hodder and Stoughton could, had they been inclined, have forwarded unopened to the printer the annual offering of, say, John Buchan or Baroness Orczy. Now authors seem to require, and certainly need, editorial changes. James Jones's novel *From Here to Eternity* clattered on for thousands of words after Pearl Harbour, and it was a percipient editor who simply guillotined it at this point. Françoise Sagan is known to have deferred totally to her editor when he required changes.

Writers, again because of their isolation, are apt to indulge in unhappy purple passages, excessive prejudices, jokes that don't come off and plots that go skidding wildly off the rails. The wise publisher should never presume to offer judgment as a connoisseur of literature, but see himself as the author's converter, in the sense that a calico printer 'converts' grey cotton cloth. He must explain to the author that he represents the public because he has to sell to the public and that it is only on these grounds, and not on questions of style, that criticisms are offered. This way they are more palatable to the author and *should* be swallowed.

* The animal in question belonged to Professor Hugh Thomas.

Loyalty and concern obviously operate in two directions, and while the author is expected to stay with his publisher, he will expect that anything he writes will be published. Every year a number of titles are put out with enormous reluctance by publishers who fear that the author might leave them if they turned a manuscript down. So they consign what they consider to be poor examples of the author's work to the printing presses rather than to the dustbin which, in a less touchy profession, would be the more appropriate place.

There are thieves in the profession – gentlemen after all can be *cabrioleurs* – and one big London publisher who should know better is notorious for writing to authors who have had a little success under a little imprint, with the suggestion that they join a bigger battalion on whose side Mammon, if not God, certainly is. Early in the author/publisher relationship, the prodigal son mentioned above rang up his publisher saying that he'd had an offer from a rival, Mr C., and what should he do? The publisher replied, 'Tell Mr C. to blank off.' The author wrote a short reply. It read: 'Dear Mr C., Blank off.' This is what is understood by an author's loyalty.

Not all authors can be trusted to behave so well, and academic historians are particularly prone to move to a publisher who can offer them access to private papers. It is galling for a publisher to nourish an author through his unprofitable years only to have him whisked away by a rival on a project which seems sure of success, but the publisher has little protection against this. He can, and indeed should, produce and insist on serious options, but no one has yet found an unbreakable one which has been tested in the courts. Better, if the author wants to leave, to say goodbye as gracefully as he can, choking back his tears. British publishers are still far from the American scene, where the publishing houses are so large that it is impossible for an author to feel loving towards them, so he becomes attached to his particular editor in the house. As the editor gyrates up the salary and power vortex, moving from publisher to publisher, so the author traipses faithfully after him, frequently leaving behind a contracted manuscript which will very likely be suffocated at birth by his editor's successor.*

In the United States the editor has replaced the publisher as understood in this book. This was dramatically illustrated by the case of *Portnoy's Complaint*, an epic of Jewish mother-love and sexual failure that quickly became a best-seller on both sides of the Atlantic in early 1969. Philip Roth approached his editor at Random House, a big publishing firm owned by an even bigger communications giant, R.C.A., and asked for an enormous ($250,000) advance on this manuscript. His editor said no, he thought that was too much, so later at a cocktail party Roth mentioned this to another Random House editor (Jason Epstein) who said, well, he thought he could try and raise the money. The money was, indeed, raised, the film rights and the paperback rights were sold rather hurriedly to take the sting out of the advance and the book became, as only the author Philip Roth had foreseen clearly, a best-seller.

Competition for literary novelists in the middle of the sales graph is relatively genteel in England, but for the guaranteed blockbuster it is savage and intense: thus, John Le Carré moved from Victor Gollancz, who originated him, to Messrs Heinemann, leaving Sir Victor muttering darkly about the misdeed, which he threatened to reveal in every detail for the general benefit of the publishing trade. Unfortunately, he did not live to do this. And in fact the reason for Le Carré's move was probably that a rival publisher bid more for his second book.†

## Authors and Ideas

The aphorism that everyone has one good book in them couldn't be less true. It's the same kind of folly as imagining that 'Letters addressed to posterity seldom reach their destination.' Of course they do, if they are properly written and carefully preserved like

* Agents are now wising up on this one and insert a provision that should an editor move on, the author has the right to repay the advance and (presumably) move on too. This is an especially necessary provision in the New York scene, of which more in Chapter 9.

† Mr Le Carré has now been secured by Hodder & Stoughton.

those of Madame de Sévigné or Schliemann. But it is a melan-
choly and daily-confirmed truth that of a thousand unsolicited
manuscripts that flow into the offices of a Second Eleven publisher,
barely one is publishable.

Ideally, the publisher should enclose a gentle note with every
returned manuscript, pointing out the defects and offering advice,
but the cost of this is so enormous that most publishers resort to
that cruellest of printed forms – the rejection slip. They must cause
pain, even when as delicately phrased as this:

56 *Doughty Street, London WC*1.
We regret having to say 'no' to your manuscript. The fact
that it proved not to our taste does not necessarily mean
your work is unpublishable, but all we can do, under the
pressure of submitted books, is to wish you better luck elsewhere.

Anthony Blond Limited

In fact, the popular, or at any rate graduate's view of publishing – that it involves reading manuscripts and pondering their
merits while twiddling a glass of sherry– is, alas, unreal. A publisher
must search out authors, projects, titles, and marry his own
ideas to the potential of a writer. It is not unheard of for even a
novel to be commissioned. *The Fourth of June* by David Benedictus and *The Feathers of Death* by Simon Raven are two typical,
successful commissioned novels. There is nothing objectionable
about this; after all, Michelangelo was commissioned to paint
the Sistine Chapel. Many creative artists prefer and enjoy direction,
criticism and even demands from a patron; they define the limits
of the work, which is half the battle in any creative activity –
witness the sonnet.

Most documentary or non-fiction titles are created by the
publisher, either out of his own head or by welding an idea
offered by an author or an agent on to one of his own. He finances
the operation which may simply consist of giving the author so
much a month, or of sending him to the other end of the world
to report on the oddities of some Amazon tribe. If anthropology

in the Lévi-Strauss vein is so fashionable, then why not use the zoologists' technique to examine our own 'civilized' behaviour? Hence *The Naked Ape* by Desmond Morris of the London Zoo.

The case of *The Naked Ape* is a classic in how to extract a work of non-fiction from a busy professional in a field other than writing, and how to promote it into the ranks of international best-sellers. It is also a good illustration of how an author can depend on his publisher for impetus and enthusiasm.

Tom Maschler, the chairman – then chief editor – of Cape, deserves a place in our portrait gallery as an entirely self-made post-war editor who has worked for publishers as various as André Deutsch and Penguin, and who has galvanized the distinguished firm founded by Jonathan Cape (himself once a traveller for Duckworth), a very fashionable imprint of the 'twenties, into one of the most alert publishers of our time. As we'll see, it all begins quite casually. Let Maschler speak:

Met Desmond Morris at a party. Fascinated by him. Not just a good talker but clearly an *original* thinker. Invited him to lunch. Had a return lunch with him at the Zoo. Over a three-year period had many many more lunches, mainly at the Zoo, where he was Curator of Mammals and too busy to come to the West End. After about a year, we began talking about *The Naked Ape* – a phrase he used casually and which I fixed on as a great title. From time to time I offered him a contract. He felt he wasn't ready to write the book – needed far more research. I pointed out that he never *would* be ready to write the book. Any little tiny piece of research would take years and even at the end of his life so much would still remain speculative. I offered him any advance he wanted, expressed as £1,000, £2,000, £3,000, £4,000, £5,000, £6,000, £7,000, £8,000, £9,000 or £10,000. Finally he agreed to write the book and chose a 'modest' advance of £3,000. Then as before, I felt and told everyone I knew that this would be the most successful book I had ever published. More lunches and about three years later, he gave me the finished first draft. It was

Christmas Eve. I called him Christmas Day having read the book, wildly excited. Long sessions of revisions followed. Mainly minor and stylistic, but some more important. Backtracking a little, I should tell you that about a year or so after our contract was signed, Desmond seemed to be spending a lot of time doing television, which I *insisted* he was doing, at least in part, for the money. In relation to my expectations for the book, it seemed like a waste of time. I asked him to do a synopsis, and wanted to place only the American rights, just to indicate to him the book's potential. I sold it to McGraw-Hill for $50,000. At that time he had published several books, none of which had sold more than about 4000 copies.

Came into the office after Christmas with the good news and began work.

First I placed the serial rights. *Observer* and *Sunday Times* interested, but not overboard. Mike Christiansen at the *Sunday Mirror* flipped. Offered ten thousand guineas and major promotion. The *Mirror* seemed to me absolutely ideal, in that I felt the book was so good that it wouldn't be 'cheapened', and we might actually reach a wider book audience. As it turned out the *Mirror* serialization was so successful that everyone you and I know seemed to be reading it. Mike Christiansen is down on record as saying it was their most successful serial ever.

Began on translation rights. Sold, for example, the German rights for $50,000 (by this time it was of course clear that the advance from McGraw-Hill was no more than a nominal fee!) Sold translation rights all over Europe and even far-off countries like Iceland, Turkey – and in Czechoslovakia not just Czech but Slovak, etc. etc. etc.

Began of course (about five months before publication) to get usual pieces in Whitefriar, *Bookseller*, etc. The *Sunday Mirror* spent a fortune hiring models to pose naked (back view) and we used their much publicized photographs for a poster, just as we suggested they use our lettering for their serial, tying in everything for maximum visual impact. Sold the paperback rights to Corgi about four months before publication for £15,000. Well before our publication the Book of the Month Club in America made the book a full selection. Graham Greene* flew over to Canada for Clarke Irwin's sales conference – just for that – *The Naked Ape* was our *big* book. Two or three months before publication we arranged for Desmond Morris to address a number of important booksellers in our offices. This is something we have only done once before and do not do lightly. In fact I'd say we'd only do it on a book by a relatively unknown (as a writer) author, and one we are confident of selling a minimum of 50,000 copies of. Sent out proofs, of course, to literary editors, etc. but *not* asking anyone for quotes. Quotes can easily alienate reviewers and must be used with great discretion. The *Sunday Mirror* serial spanned our publication and Desmond was easy, I admit it, to get on a dozen television programmes; the acclaim, the sales, the rest, is history.

Tom Maschler wrote this account at my behest for this book. It is, as he mentioned in the covering letter, in 'shorthand', but remark the enthusiasm, remark the persistence, and remark the success. *The Naked Ape* was just right for Dr Desmond Morris and Dr Desmond Morris was just right for *The Naked Ape*. Which brings us on to the question of finding an author for an idea.

After 1945 there was a short breathing-space during which travel books became popular in the Western world, but then the war started again in publishers' lists and the first editor to think of finding out the former enemy's point of view was a trend-setter. *The Von Papen Memoirs*, from a surviving Nazi, and *A Biography of Rommel* by Desmond Young quickly succeeded each other, and it was left to owner-driver publisher William Kimber to dig out some Japanese and Italian admirals. Then came another fashion – disasters: *A Night to Remember* (Walter Lord) was the

---

* Known in the trade as Graham C. Greene to distinguish him from his uncle.

brainchild of an American editor, Howard Cady. It was a block-buster.

Often in these cases it is the publisher who has to sell the author the idea, guarantee him his living and expenses, and arrange his research. The book may not echo in the Halls of Fame, but it will be a pleasing mixture of instruction and entertainment. Those authors who can exploit the middle-brow passion for information seasoned with excitement are the real professionals: they may not be so amusing as the wholly imaginative writers of novels, but a publisher's list must be balanced between the two general areas of fiction and non-fiction and bookmaking of quality produces steady sellers and is unlikely to let the publisher down.

## Authors' Rewards

The average author (Desmond Morris was just this with his sales of four thousand copies before *The Naked Ape*) does not fear the hot breath of the income tax inspector down his neck. But so much money tumbled into Dr Morris's lap from the sales of *The Naked Ape* that he had to hie himself to Malta for a year to avoid the exigencies of British income tax. In Gozo he could have bumped into a similarly skulking Hunter Davies, whose book on the Beatles had been sold to the American publishers McGraw-Hill for $100,000 just a few months before.

Under our taxation system a suddenly enriched author is treated not much better than a lucky bookmaker, worse than a Pools winner; unlike a trainer of horses, he cannot regard the sales of rights as a capital gain, nor can it be tax free as with bloodstock. It is particularly galling because, quite often, an author only has one hit in a lifetime and for this fortunate experience, which may never be repeated, he is only allowed to slide his earnings over three years.

There is one interesting dodge, however, whereby a lucky and best-selling author may convert income into capital. Booker Brothers, the Trinidad traders and donors of the biggest literary prize in Britain, will occasionally 'buy' a young author who has

c

caught their enlightened eye, exchanging a handsome, relatively low-taxed capital sum for his earnings for life or for a period of years.

The current tax chieftain of Ireland, a Mr Haughey, inspired by the Anglo-American author Constantine Fitzgibbon, has decreed that there shall be a Renaissance in the Republic: all artists and writers whose output is of artistic merit – whatever that may mean – will be allowed to live in his country without paying a ha'porth of tax.* This might be going too far, but it is surely arguable that authors should not be put on a par with people whose earning power is unrelated to the skill of their creative imagination. All a publisher can do in these circumstances is find his lucky author a good accountant and wave him goodbye.

## Choosing a Manuscript and an Author

Before deciding to offer a contract, a publisher will ask of himself the following sort of questions: (1) Is the book worth publishing (why, and who's going to buy it?). (2) Is the book well-written? (3) If not, can it be improved by the author or by an outside hand? (4) Will it sell? (5) If not, will it be of such literary prestige or importance as to reflect glory on our house? (6) Where did it come from? (Publishers in the first stages of even reading a manuscript pay a great deal of attention to its source; there is a certain kind of agent who sends out certain kinds of books, whose only apparent purpose is collecting a fat enough dossier of rejection slips to impress his American client.) (7) What are we going to sell the paperback rights for, or aren't we? (8) Is there a film in it, a serial? (9) Will the Americans like it? (10) Can we sell it to the *Observer*, the *Sunday Mirror*, *Lady's Home Journal*, or whatever? (11) What about the author, is this a one-shot book? (Remember we publish authors and not manuscripts.) (12) Has the author stamina? (13) Is he or she well-connected? Too well-connected (i.e. liable to be a pain in the neck)? (14) Can we afford the price the agent is asking? (15) Do we want any more

* Mr Len Deighton has now settled in Ireland.

books this year, next year, some time or ever? (16) Is it on a subject that has been rather overdone lately, e.g. homosexuality, LSD, black backlash in the States, emergent African countries, Wigan Lad Makes Good, etc.? (17) Is the book obscene or defamatory? If so, to what extent? (It is the duty of a lawyer to warn his client the publisher of possible consequences of publication; a wise publisher can then decide what risks to take with the benefit of that advice.)

If most of these questions can be answered cheerfully, the publisher may proceed. There are many wrong reasons for publishing a book, and here are some of them: (1) The author threatens to go elsewhere. (2) The doors of a great country house will be flung open to the publisher if this particular dreary Memoir of an Edwardian Childhood can be led on its way to the remainder dealers. (3) The publisher was under the dentist's drill when he agreed to this particular history of that profession. (4) The publisher's appendix was taken out by a friend of the author's thirty years ago.* (5) It is the autobiography of the head of an African state – be careful, as it usually takes nine months to produce a book from manuscript and nine months is a long time in the life of an African politician. (6) If you do her poems, I think we can get her away from Heinemann. (7) Vanity – George (Weidenfeld) wants it.

In the politics of publishing these reasons are not so silly and resistible as they sound. But if a publisher doesn't respect himself, who else will?

---

* It has been observed that wrong reasons (3) and (4) are frivolous. Maybe, but the incidents are true and only discretion forbids my naming the two titles now in print.

# 3

## Literary Agents

Agents were originally called into being by the rapacity of publishers: Grant Richards, for example, bought the copyright of *The Ragged Trousered Philanthropists* – that Edwardian best-seller – outright for £25; Tressell's widow had the occasional ex gratia payment, but she would have been better off with a royalty contract.

The function of an agent is to sell, nourish and promote his clients' works: a good agent will act as both buffer and lubricant between the author and publisher, explaining to each the other's view, and is treasured by both parties; quite often a publisher who senses temperament in a new author will actually procure him an agent in self-defence. A good agent will be pliant yet firm with his clients, as well as with the publisher; above all, he will be straight. Most of the sixty-four agents listed in *The Writers' and Artists' Year Book* are conscientious and honest, but certain agents will knowingly represent unreliable clients, like those who take advances from publishers with no intention of delivering a manuscript.

An agent will rarely have a contract with an author,* and certainly never with a publisher. He (or often she) will have his or her favourite publishers, but a very close bond between a

* A literary agent is better protected financially than the publisher. His right to 10 per cent of the author's proceeds is inalienable and must be paid whether his agency is mentioned in the contract or not (always provided it can be proved that he or she sold the book). This was established in 1926 over the Sax Röhmer case.

publisher and an agent can be dangerous for the agent since it restricts his known selling range. However, despite the absence of a contract, the relationship between author and agent is so intimate that if the author deserts his agent's banner the loss is felt much more deeply than if he had left his publisher.

An agent is valuable to a publisher, first as a filter, and secondly as a source. A book submitted by an agent will presumably have achieved a certain level of literacy and competence, and so most publishers will at least have them read. Publishers quickly learn to discriminate between the offerings of a large agency which is more of a wholesale grocer than a literary factor, and those of the hard-working agent who has actually read the manuscripts he is offering. A letter like this does not help anybody:

Dear Mr Rosencrantz,★
   THIRD TIME LUCKY by N. B. Gooseberry
We have much pleasure in submitting this and look forward
to your offer for the British and Commonwealth rights.
                                  Yours, etc.

Who is N. B. Gooseberry? Young or old, male or female, pseudonymous, or, unbelievably, real? Is it a novel or the story of his attempt to invent a one-man hovercraft? Or what? Better would be a letter like this:

Dear Rosencrantz,
   THIRD TIME LUCKY by N. B. Gooseberry
As I told you over the telephone this morning, Noel Gooseberry really does exist, all eighteen stone of him, and
Gooseberry really is his name. He keeps a pub in that most
calamitous of all British resorts, Bognor Regis (weren't
George V's dying words 'Damn Bognor Regis'?), and this is
a story of smuggling on the Sussex coasts through the
centuries. He seems to have been to a great deal of trouble

★ Of the firm Rosencrantz & Guildenstern Ltd, invented by Michael Turner, Desmond Briggs and Desmond Elliott (all q.v.) for skits at the Society of Young Publishers.

with eighteenth-century newspapers, collating old wives' tales, and he brings the story rather staggeringly up to date. Did you know that quite a lot of West End bars get brandy in kegs illegally from France even now? I think he's a most amusing character, an absolute Grandma Moses of a writer, and I do look forward to your reaction.

Yours, etc.

P.S. I loathe the title don't you?

Here is a warm-hearted, informative, tempting letter. Something will have to be done.

A publisher enjoys dealing with an agent who sounds him out before sending a book in, is not extortionate in his demands, is honest about the past history of the book and the author (i.e. how many people have seen it and said 'no'? Is he a drunk, a lunatic or a bankrupt?) and will protect the publisher if need be from the author. Some authors like to design their own jacket, insist on knowing the print order and the type face, ring up furiously from Didcot complaining that the local Smith's is not stocking their book, demand to know weekly sales figures, or use the publisher's office as a poste restante or a laundry. From all these tendencies they should be diverted by a firm agent and, in return, the publisher will probably push the odd client his or her way.

An agency should admit its weaknesses, too. Not all of the sixty-four London agents are equally proficient in the film, dramatic, television, Japanese or other markets in which a book can be exploited. Moreover, a good agent will realize that if he persuades a publisher to overpay an author, and the book loses money, he is imperilling his client's future. There is nothing more difficult to hawk around than a manuscript which has been turned down by the author's first publisher. It's like a discarded Member of Parliament looking for a seat.

Publishers in the First Eleven rely more heavily on agents to fill their lists than those in the Second, who cannot fairly bank on being offered first look at the fruits of an agent's orchard. An agent with a riveting pictorial study of *A Day in the Life of an Ai* (a useful word in Scrabble and also a three-toed sloth from South America) would be foolish if he did not first offer it to Mr Collins, well-known for his love of animal-kind.* Again, an agent handling a blockbuster from the United States will probably, unless it has some peculiar distinction or is unusually obscene, canvass first the big, established houses like Cassells, Heinemann, Collins and A.B.P. who, if they care to, can pull out the stops with greater effectiveness than their colleagues in the Second Eleven. To that extent a publishing giant can sit still and wait for agents to come forward with their wares, whereas the Second Eleven publisher, often a post-war house, must be a great deal more creative. The smaller the publisher, the less interested he is in the bigger agents and they in him.

However, an agent with young ideas may be more attracted and better received by a small publishing house than a large; and furthermore, the wise agent must remember that some smaller houses are known for their ability occasionally to squeeze the lemon until the pips squeak. In 1951 a new agent sent out a general letter inviting interviews from publishers. The most polite reply came from Messrs Paul Elek and it was to this small house that the agent offered his first book. *Boldness Be My Friend* by Richard Pape, M.M., was the first prisoner-of-war story from the pen of 'another rank'. Elek pounced on it and sold sixty thousand copies. It is doubtful whether a bigger publishing firm would have sold a tenth of this. Thus perhaps another proposition can be deduced: small firms care more; they have more to gain and more to lose. An agent should be aware of this, and capable of sensing the different tastes and susceptibilities of the entire publishing spectrum.

No author should be too downcast if an agent refuses to handle his book or work. They have their blind spots too. A young man in his first job with an agent once lost what was thought to be a crucial letter. His furious employer insisted that he spend the whole weekend looking through the files until he found it. He

* Collins have indeed published a pictorial life of the three-toed sloth.

didn't find it, but he did come across a letter which read something like this:

Dear Mr Osborne,
### LOOK BACK IN ANGER
I regret that after reading your play we have come to the conclusion that it has no commercial value.

Yours, etc.

# 4

## How to Produce Books

In the Gutenberg Museum at Mainz there is a reconstruction of the world's first printing press. One man is picking out type, another is fixing the paragraphs into wedges, another screwing the forme on to the press; it is inked and lowered on to paper and the wet sheet is hung up for drying. When the paper is dried the sixteen- (or thirty-two-) page sheets are folded, collated, stitched together and bound.

In letterpress printing, which is the cheapest for print runs of around two thousand books with up to 16 pages of plates, much the same procedure is followed today. There are a variety of types to choose from and the printing machine is electrically powered; otherwise the same sort of simple, if fiddly business continues.

Printers are bigger, fewer and richer than publishers, and very few publishers apart from the university presses, Hutchinson and Collins have their own printing press. Inevitably, because of the endemic charm and optimism of the publisher and the credulity mixed with greed of the printer, printers end up by owning publishers. This is how Walter Hutchinson amassed his collection of publishing houses and, so keen was he to keep his presses running, he once seized a pile of rejected manuscripts and sent them to his printers.

The credit offered by a printer to a publisher will be, at the worst, thirty days, much more likely ninety, and all too often it drifts drowsily off into the sands of time and deeper indebtedness.

Publishers are constantly hopeful and printers, with their expensive machinery tying up capital, ever loath to lose an order. This false optimism placed the Purnell group of printers (now part of the British Printing Corporation conglomerate) in a position to acquire Macdonald, Sampson Low and Max Parrish.

Publishers, with very little capital apart from their office equipment, can lose their heads, pay far too much for a book, print far too many and sell far too few. This trap must be avoided by the wily publisher. The trouble is that while at the moment of acquisition a property, like a potential Derby winner, may seem to be on winning form, in between contract and publication the animal develops asthma, or it becomes clear that the publisher has over-estimated its stamina. We have seen how before the war, Nicholson & Watson went down over Lloyd George's memoirs, for which they paid forty thousand pounds. The respectable firm of Constable, in which their printer Hutchinson's now have a substantial minority share, overprinted Lord Moran's reminiscences to the tune of fifty thousand copies, which they sold off at a 'special' price, and even Hutchinson's as publishers can catch a cold, as they did with Svetlana Alliluyeva's *Twenty Letters to a Friend*, printing a hundred thousand copies of which barely a third sold.

Unfortunately, the kind of self-induced optimism, amounting sometimes to hysteria, which produces such grandiose advances and print orders is infectious, and there has yet to be a printer who has quietly offered doubts as to the wisdom of spoiling so many tons of clean white paper with so many gallons of ink. A wise publisher should remember, first, that it is always possible to reprint a book running well, and, second, that no publisher ever went broke on the books he *didn't* print (though in a fashionable, fast-thinking title with a short selling life he might lose profit by going early out of print).

The economics of printing – the cost per copy, the best print run – are, briefly, murderous, as a simple division sum will show: about 30,000 titles are published every year in Great Britain, yielding only £150,000,000. So the business of printing a book is, in terms of money, a small one; and besides, the materials involved are fiddly and not reusable in the same form. One can only conclude that a good printer will stake a new publisher if he has confidence in him. Printers still stand in their relation to publishers somewhat as a Bond Street trader does to a deb. She may be flighty and not know her own mind but she is a customer, and she could be well-enough connected to pay.

The design and appearance of a general book matter, but not too much; after all, printing is only a form of communication and rarely an end in itself. A book should be readable and clean, and the design should not obtrude to the extent that it distracts the reader from the author's thoughts. Cognoscenti of type-face can finnick for hours over whether a certain typescript should be set in Caslon Old-Face, which does not reproduce very well by offset or rotogravure; or Imprint, a type specially cut in 1912 which is an open squared-out and larger-face version of Caslon; or Bodoni, which is rather elegant and powerful and was the type used most appropriately by the publishers of Mervyn Peake's Gothic novel *Titus Groan*; or Bembo, which is a cheerful, open, late-fifteenth-century face; but the ordinary book will probably end up in Baskerville, a nice middle-of-the-road sort of type-face that nobody particularly notices, or Plantin – and if you can tell the difference, you're a better man than I. Nobody has yet returned a book to a bookshop on the grounds that it was printed in Baskerville 11/12 instead of Bembo 14 point.

One publisher was asked by the Society of Young Publishers what he did about production in his tiny set-up, and replied, 'I say to the printer, make it look like a Cape book.' There was some derisive laughter, but in fact a good printer produces a good-looking book, and a bad printer a bad one. A small publisher will either trust the printer completely and leave it up to him, or hire somebody to deal with production – a production manager. It will be the production manager's job to choose among the printers who solicit business from him or her, decide who offers the best quotation and place the appropriate order. He or she will deal with paper merchants, printers, binders and even the brass makers, who produce the lettering on the spine of the book, and that little design which we call the 'colophon'.

O.U.P.  Heinemann Educational  Cassell  Jonathan Cape

It will be better if the production manager concentrates on a few printers simply because it is easier to deal with one printer and twenty books rather than twenty printers with one book each.\* He will also beware of trendy, foreign printers and of complicated deals where the film-setting is done in Hong Kong, the origination in Malta and the machining in Italy: they nearly always generate language problems, even when done on a massive and continuous scale as innovated by Paul Hamlyn in Czechoslovakia and Captain Maxwell in East Germany.† Anyway, devaluation has taken some of the charm and a lot of the business from foreign printers.

The process of converting a typescript into a few thousand copies of a book is still one of the simplest in manufacturing today. Let us take this book – the one you are looking at now – and see how it was made. It consists of ink, paper, adhesive, thread, boards and fabric, and is, or was, covered with a paper jacket.

It began as a messy typescript with many corrections, and some passages (of which this was one) written in longhand. It was retyped in double spacing and two copies sent to the publisher, or more exactly to an editor within the house, who, after requiring emendations, passed it on to the production department. The pro-

---

\* It is equally dangerous for a publisher to deal with one printer only; the latter is bound to assume an overbearing-creditor position, as we have seen was the case with Walter Hutchinson and Wilfred Harvey of Purnell's, now B.P.C.

† Thousands of a Pergamon Press primary English catalogue had to be returned to East Germany because the opening line ran, 'My name ist Wilhemina.'

duction department made a rough estimate of its length – and it was not a straightforward operation, like the average novel of 60,000 words which makes 224 pages, because this book has line blocks, tables, appendices and footnotes, and on occasion breaks into different type sizes. The cast-off, which is a character count, enables you to work out accurately how many printed pages the book will make. Frequently the production manager will send the manuscript to the printer to have this calculation done, and the printer will also set up a specimen page and produce an estimate. Several printers may prepare estimates for the same manuscript, and the production manager will give the job to the favoured printer. In the case of this book, it was sent to Butler & Tanner Ltd, Frome and London, where it was tapped out on a keyboard by the compositor (known as a 'comp'), Mr Antell. This particular book was set in Monotype. It took the comp 72 hours to produce a roll of perforated paper which was fed into a Monotype caster: air is blown through the perforations, causing letters made of an alloy of lead, tin and antimony to be selected in the same way as notes are selected for the keyboard of a pianola. (Hollerith borrowed this principle from the Jacquard loom to father the computer.)

The assembled letters (the 'type') were slotted into slender trays or 'galleys' (U.S. 'slides') and inked, and paper was rolled over them to produce galley proofs. Galley proofs are strips of paper the width of one page and the length of approximately three pages. The printer's reader read the galleys and corrected the compositor's errors and as many of mine as he could spot. A proof-reader, the editor and I then checked the galleys, changed the text here and there (an expensive and tedious business – second thoughts are not to be encouraged) and sent them back to the printer for make up into pages. Then 'page' or 'book' proofs were produced for a double check. These resemble a paperback book. Nowadays, most uncomplicated typescripts proceed directly to page proof, omitting the stage of showing the galleys to the author for correction. At book-proof stage only the smallest of alterations should be made, since the type has now been made up into pages; the deletion or addition of even a few lines could mean that a whole chapter had to be re-paged.

Look carefully at the bottom left-hand corner of pages 17, 33, 49, etc., of this book and you will find a capital letter. Each one indicates the beginning of a new 'section'. If you are really roused, rip apart the covers and you will see little black marks stretching diagonally across the 'spine'. These indicate the order in which the sections have to be bound. All this helps the binder to collate the sheets accurately.

Before this book was printed, but when its extent and thickness were known, work was started on the jacket. The design was chosen and the final artwork, together with the blurb, were sent to a different printer who delivered his product to the binder for wrapping round the completed job.

It is sometimes difficult to justify to impatient authors, their agents and even their editors within a publishing house why the time between delivery of the typescript and publication is so long – between six and nine months. For the basic ingredients of book production – composing, machining and binding – do not take long: a book can be produced in three weeks with everybody working round the clock. But why should they? The proper production of a book is both a stately and a cumbersome process. The construction of the 'prelims', i.e. the preliminary pages before the main text, often given roman numerals, is exacting. If an index is required, an indexer must be found, and one frequently has to queue for a good one. Proofs have to be checked by the author and the editor, and should, if the publishing house is conscientious, be checked again by an outside proofreader. The jacket is crucial, since it is the only strictly 'packaging' item in the production of a book; it will probably be the responsibility of a separate department which, having screwed the blurb out of the editor, has to find an appropriate designer who will submit sketches which might not please the sales department ... and so on. Then there is the trade advertising and booksellers' information servicing.

Publishers are constantly getting their dates wrong and this is mainly because they don't allow themselves enough time. If the book has to come out quickly, it should probably never be published in hard covers at all. Norah Smallwood, a director of Chatto & Windus – until recently one of the last partnerships in London – said, 'I refuse to publish a book which has not been in the catalogue twice.' She meant by this that the 'subscription' (q.v.) for a title matures, like wine, only with time, and this is what Chatto's agents from London to Auckland must have on their side, especially for the smaller, infrequently visited book outlets (see pp. 52–3).

# 5

## How to Sell Books

Your favourite *tante à heritage* is being dried out at an expensive drunks' home in Wiltshire. She is an avid reader of literary journals and you know that in her quieter moment she likes the odd first novel. You have read excellent reviews of *It Happened on Sunday* by Frederick de Poobah (Rosencrantz & Guildenstern, £1·95) in *The Times Literary Supplement*, the *Listener*, the *New Statesman*, the *Spectator*, *New Society*, the *Sunday Times*, the *Sunday Telegraph*, the *Observer* and so forth. You enter a branch of W. H. Smith in Andover, Hungerford, Shaftesbury or wherever you may be. You pass through the entrance which is banked by paperbacks, skirt a large table covered with Books for Pleasure, marked ORIGINALLY PUBLISHED AT 5 GUINEAS, NOW ONLY £2·75, and move to the recesses of the shop among the Olivettis, last year's diaries and some gramophone records, to discover the bookshelves. On the shelves you notice copies of Beatrix Potter, Mrs Beeton, *The Observer Book of Worms*, some dictionaries from Cassells, Oxford and Collins, a book about a tame lion, some Oxford Classics, a row of Teach Yourself books published by English University Press, a row of Everyman books published by Dent, collected editions of Somerset Maugham from Messrs Heinemann, the odd novel by C. P. Snow, some gardening books from Messrs Collingridge and a stack of Ladybirds. A row of Blackie's juveniles at 47½p, and that's it. You are now an observer of the British book trade.

It is not the fault of the much-satirized, near-monopoly W. H.

Smith that they haven't got *It Happened on Sunday*, published by Rosencrantz & Guildenstern at £1·95 and widely reviewed. It is rather the fault of the British public, which spends about one pound per head, per annum, on books compared with three pounds in Holland, four pounds in Norway and New Zealand and seven pounds in the United States. Even when we make allowance for the fact that these figures were published in a 1967 report, and take into account the relative standards of living and earning in these countries, the conclusion must be that the British public do not love books. Or, rather, they do not buy many books. The books you see around you are those of worth proven over decades, and are not for book buyers but for people who occasionally need a book. *Winnie-the-Pooh* is reprinted in swathes of fifty thousand copies. *Little Black Sambo* must have sold in the millions; even the children of atheists are regularly confirmed and need a Bible to mark the event; and younger children are avid readers and are still happy with *Black Beauty* if they are girls, or Percy F. Westerman if they are boys. Sturdy, unobjectionable, often informative books like these are the basis of a publisher's prosperity; it is difficult for a new publisher to manufacture such an item and his main hope is for a best-seller.

'Have you', you ask a sixteen-year-old assistant in a green smock, 'a copy of *It Happened on Sunday*? I believe it has just come out.' The girl looks so frightened that you fear she may faint into your arms, and bolts behind a case full of Parker Pens. There emerges a much fiercer-looking lady with a bun and a much neater green smock. 'Can I help you?' (as if dealing with a trespasser).

'Yes, I was wondering if you have a copy of *It Happened on Sunday* by Frederick de Poobah, published by Rosencrantz & Guildenstern at £1·95?'

'Are you the author, then?' The lady has been a long time in the game and knows that anybody so well informed is likely to be. 'I'm afraid we don't stock R. & G.'s books, and we never see their traveller. I could get it for you, though,' she adds. The truth is that she has seen the book, which she remembers as having **a** mildly obscene jacket, but being a sensible lady she knows that her chances of selling even one copy are slight. She does see Rosencrantz & Guildenstern's traveller, whom she rather likes, and always makes a point of accepting his offer of a cup of coffee, but, generally speaking, they don't have the sort of books she can sell in Andover, Malmesbury, Salisbury, Shaftesbury or wherever she is. Nevertheless, she is prepared not to let the side (W. H. Smith) down. You plump instead for an entire set of Beatrix Potter, exquisite value at 42½p and with the original artwork still as fresh as a daisy.

The poor R. & G. salesman had parked his two-year-old Morris 1000 in the town square and called on The Book-Worm and the local W. H. Smith's branch, carrying his heavy 'splad' – containing dust-jackets of all their spring wares – but he knew that in spite of the promises he'd heard at the sales conference of good reviews for *It Happened on Sunday*, in this particular town, with this particular title, and despite the conventionally sordid jacket (a mixture of crumpled sheets and naked bodies) he wouldn't really stand a chance. He quite understood the buyer's reluctance to place an order, and knew that in this little market town Smith's did not supply the public library, and so could not order even one copy on the off-chance that an esoteric reader might demand one from that source of free reading matter. Everyone had tried; what had gone wrong? The answer is that the British don't love books enough.

Supposing you had persisted in your request for one copy of *It Happened on Sunday* by Frederick de Poobah, published by Rosencrantz & Guildenstern at £1·95. In the first place you are unusual; the average customer wouldn't get all these details right; why should he? All he knows is that an amusing novel by some-body with a ridiculous name was published by a firm with an even sillier name and that it was something to do with sex in Baden-Baden. With these clues a conscientious bookseller may scan the bibliography put out once a week in the *Bookseller*, or, if really bright, look at the reviews. It is in fact essential to know the name of the publisher or the author. This discovered and the order taken (some book shops wisely insist on a deposit, because they may never see this literature-hungry customer again) it would go off to the publisher. As you chose to order your book on Friday afternoon at 3.30, the order would be posted on Monday and received on Tuesday in the afternoon post, too late for the morning's 'editing', or sorting out of orders: Rosencrantz & Guildenstern are quite up to the minute and use the publishers' computer service at Neasden, so someone has to 'edit' the order, which means putting a string of numbers on it, identifying it from the other hundreds of thousands of books that pass through Book Centre's hands in the year.

On Wednesday morning the edited order is collected by a little van and driven off to Neasden. The computing machine, which looks like an enormous deep-freeze, big enough for a liner, with a typewriter keyboard as a tailpiece, searches its electronic memory and from the information provided produces an invoice on an impressive form which is equally capable of invoicing £20,000-worth or 80p-worth of books. The form gives the following information: the International Standard Book Number (I.S.B.N.) of the book, running into ten digits; the account number of the publisher; the account number of the bookseller and the discount* he is accorded (this ranges from $16\frac{2}{3}$ per cent to $36\frac{1}{4}$ per cent in the U.K.); the area in which the book was ordered so that the appropriate traveller may eventually collect commission (if he is working on commission). The computer 'extends the invoice', i.e. works out the discount; and, finally, adds that it was a home and not an export sale – there is a differential in royalties payable to the author. All this at a cost of 4p. The invoice is then sent off to the R. & G. warehouse, which is situated just behind the railway station in Bromley next to a disused ice-cream store.

By this time it is Friday. If the warehouseman is conscientious, he will look out the book from among Rosencrantz & Guildenstern's 250-odd titles, pack it up and send it by book post to the

---

* 'Discounts' and 'terms' are the main source of friction between publishers and booksellers. The Joint Working Party set up by the two Associations recommended the establishment of one discount of 35 per cent on all titles plus a service charge of 15 per cent on orders worth less than £3. Such simplicity is unlikely to gain universal acceptance.

book shop, where it will be received on the following Monday, opened up perhaps that afternoon, and sit with a little slip awaiting your return. For heaven's sake *do* go back and collect it; otherwise all this labour will have been profitless. It will by now be clear why publishers discourage what they call 'single-copy' orders.

Now let's play this operation the other way round. It is just possible that Miss Prendergast, the buyer at W. H. Smith's in … wherever it is, is confident in the salesman's recommendation of this particular unappetizing first novel, and at the back of her mind knows very well that they have a customer in an advertising agent with a country cottage nearby who likes to pop in on the occasional naughty, intelligent first novel. So she says yes, she does want a copy of this book, and the happy salesman has 'subscribed' a copy of *It Happened on Sunday* by Frederick de Poobah, published by Rosencrantz & Guildenstern. This transaction is achieved by a salesman showing only a jacket, which in a well ordered publishing house should be available at least four months before publication for precisely this purpose; it is unlikely that Miss Prendergast, however conscientious, will ever read the book; if she read every book she bought, she'd go blind.

Today's 'subscription' system is a pleasant relic from the eighteenth-century method of placing books with the Publick in advance of publication. Dr Johnson subscribed twenty thousand copies of his *Dictionary* in this way and it must have been surely intended as a sort of advance subsidy, rather like subscription balls used to be; presumably if there were not enough subscriptions there was no book or no ball. In the case of some ruthless American publishers this still happens. A book's existence will be 'promised' by an advance jacket from an editor, and if the subscription doesn't warrant publication the book will be abandoned (and so too, eventually, will its editor). After all, the publisher does not enter into a contract with *anybody* ever to supply the space between the dust covers, as they used to be called.

The subscription system needs time to work properly. All too often the excitable publisher turns out a jacket a few weeks before publication. If he could wait a few months, or even a year, he would find that his agents from New Zealand to Cape Town, Trinidad, Toronto, Wigan and Belfast, would have time to collect orders. In fact some of the most profitable books are those which have been left rusting with their jackets as quiet heralds tooting their imminence all over the world. When an old-established publisher declares that he hasn't a free spot on his list for two years, he is either being polite about the qualities of the book he is being offered, or feels that its chances are so dim that it must stay in the catalogue and have its jacket circulated for a long time in order to snowball.

Further, the subscription system provides a guide for the print number. Up until the late 1950s it was possible with the un-exceptional book – as most books are – to say that if the sub-scription was 1,000 copies the print order should be 3,000, and if the subscription was 3,000 the print order should be 9,000, plus one for the pot and so forth. Now that booksellers either operate a severe, if intelligent, stock-control system, or are so short of capital that they cannot afford to invest or commit themselves on anything but a certainty, subscription figures are lower and become uncertain guides. Further, the difference between 'journey' (i.e. terms offered by a traveller when soliciting an order) and 'post' (i.e. what happens when a customer walks in and orders a book that is not in stock), are not yet dramatic enough to entice booksellers to take a bit of a gamble together with a publisher.

The publishing trade, anyway, runs counter to the efficient atmosphere of a mass-marketing and mass-production world. We are, as stated before, engaged in producing far too many books in far too limited quantities. We are not using the printing machine to its best ability. In the U.K., public demand is diminishing but the annual number of titles is not. To this extent, publishers are inefficient: gloriously so, in that who can say, until a book is published, whether it is a work of art or a with-it ephemera? A title may endure a hundred years; it may be recognized in a generation's time; or it may be stillborn from the press. The publishing trade's destiny of running against the economic tide is not helped by the individualism* on both sides of the trade: on the one hand, publishers insist on the right to offer books for sale at a variety of terms, ranging from $16\frac{2}{3}$ per cent to 60 per cent (in the case of far-off climes), with various conditions applying to carriage forward, carriage backward, extra discounts on special orders, and so on; on the other hand, booksellers insist on sending orders which vary from long wiggly strips of paper with the order number carefully concealed under a large staple, to the enormous documents, like writs, favoured by Blackwell's. It is time that booksellers and publishers accepted simpler terms of trade and standardized orders and invoices. At any given time a committee will be sitting earnestly trying to rationalize the book trade, and at the time of writing the author is on the current body. But until both the Booksellers' and the Publishers' Associations are given authority by their members, nothing can be done to discipline their natural eccentricities.

The publisher who considers the chore of selling books beneath him will not last long. One well-loved figure of the book trade is reported to have entered the revolving door of a Folkestone Hotel where the Booksellers' Conference was being held, to have taken one horrified glance through his eyeglass at the horde, and continued with his circular progress out again. He went bust. Even the most exalted figures in the trade take a keen interest in the business of selling. The formidable, the athletic Billy Collins was seen between safaris, pushing a bookseller in Nairobi into ordering up from Collins. Victor Weybright, the plump and immensely successful American co-founder of The New American Library, records with some pride that while whizzing back to London to buy the reprint rights of *Doctor Zhivago*, he sold one copy of every title in his Mentor list at a Khartoum bookshop.† And Sir

---

* The same Working Party (see note p. 51) has also suggested standardizing invoices and order forms.

† Victor Weybright, *The Making of a Publisher* (Weidenfeld & Nicolson, London, 1969). Although the British do not love books, they are intrigued by publishers. It is odd that this title, which was almost entirely about the American book trade, sold much better in this country than in America.

Stanley Unwin was famous for his energy in places as far apart as Vancouver and New South Wales.

A publisher obviously has more chance of selling his wares to a bookshop, or indeed to a school, if they are in the hands of a human being, than via the most dynamic form of mail-order putsch. While only 10 per cent of the bookshops in this country sell 80 per cent of the books published, it is important that these outlets be visited regularly and that the salesman the book buyer sees is truly the representative of the publisher. He should, there-fore, be honest, clean and sober – booksellers tend to be low church in their affections – he should care about books, be a 'bookman' in fact, and he should be trusted by the publisher. If these qualifications are satisfied, the publisher should be well served.

Lest it be thought that the business of distributing books is dreary, over-complicated and concerned with peanuts, let us turn to the promotion of the best-seller, which so beatifically illu-minates what is normally a pretty stolid show.

The only reliable gauge of a best-seller is an author's royalty statement. Guides to what books are selling are published regularly by *Smith's Trade News* (though not, significantly enough, by that more august journal of our trade, the *Bookseller*, which does so only at Christmas); occasionally by the *Evening News*, the *Evening Standard*, the *Sunday Express* and the *Sunday Telegraph*, and monthly by the *Sunday Times*. None of these reflects accurately the position of titles on the charts; the survey is too arbitrary a sample and the booksellers who send in their suggestions are often tempted to list books which they have bought in deeply, rather than those which are actually moving. Today's British home-market best-seller is a pretty shorn lamb. Whereas thirty years ago a sale of eighty thousand could be chalked up, now a sale of ten thousand is accepted as belonging to the best-seller category. This diminution is due to the increase in free issues by public libraries, now five hundred million books a year, and the unwillingness of the public to pay £1·95 or £2·50 for a novel which they know will be available to them in paperback within two years at 30p or 20p. A book becomes a best-seller when people can't wait for the paperback.

The weekly best-seller lists are particularly unreliable and it has been known for a London paper to list as a best-seller a book which has sold less than 1,100 copies. The *Sunday Times*'s monthly survey is more trustworthy, but in England there is nothing approaching the sweep and detail of the *Publishers' Weekly* analysis, which gives the numbers of copies in print (American publishers are much more forthcoming in this and every other way with information), the number of weeks the book has appeared, its last week's position, percentage of sales and sales in local areas. Comparison between the two countries shows that an American best-seller probably starts at fifty thousand and can go to 500,000; in England very few titles sell in these quantities any more. We are an electorate of 25,000,000 stingy book buyers. America, with five times our population, is a nation of generous book buyers – if conformist ones. The American public is more sensitive to success and more frightened of not being 'with-it'. In America a practice exists (known as 'hyping' in the record business) whereby a film company which has acquired the rights in a title forces it on to the best-seller list by sending young publicity men around armed with hundred-dollar bills and instructions to buy twenty or more copies from selected book shops. This practice has not yet reached this country. However, a film company can put a book on the best-seller list – as was the case with that excellent novel *The Manchurian Candidate* – but it cannot keep it there: that is up to the public, who may not co-operate.

Best-sellers come in two categories: automatic and unexpected. The automatic are generally the third or even the thirtieth offering of an established writer. The automatic best-sellers of post-war England have nearly always been the automatic best-sellers of pre-war England. Graham Greene, Georgette Heyer, Daphne du Maurier, Compton Mackenzie, Rebecca West *et al.* are a great deal more reliable as income earners for a publisher than Kingsley Amis, Simon Raven or even Edna O'Brien. This reflects the fact that the biggest reading section of the public – aged between fifty and seventy – are also the biggest book buyers. The British public is as loyal to revered authors as they are to Dames in the theatre. No matter what play Edith Evans or Sybil Thorndike is billed in the public will turn up through the sleet to see her. No matter what Daphne du Maurier writes in her special manner, reminiscent, as one acid young reviewer said, of 'mulled galleons', thirty thousand people will buy copies. Daphne du Maurier is a publisher's dream. He doesn't have to worry what the reviewers say, he checks his last sales to get the print order, he doesn't mind paying a high royalty of even 20 per cent; and, very important, he knows that the first print should sell out and that he will never have to remainder – the expense and agony of publishing lies in the warehouse, those books which are as immovable as the Rock of Gibraltar and much less controversial.

The launching, engineering, discovery, invention or whatever of the unexpected best-seller is not so unplanned as it looks. The publisher who has prepared this offering for the general public will have gone to great pains to make sure that its excellence is capable of being recognized. It is in this area that imprint counts. For instance the trade – the *public* are indifferent to the imprint – would not expect or accept a big romantic novel from Messrs Calder and Boyars, and it would be surprised if Messrs Dent were to claim the discovery of a new brilliant British, Kingsley-Amis-type author – although oddly enough Dent, of the Everyman Library, published Dylan Thomas. All this is unfair, but the trade is slow to recognize changes in a publisher's image, as many have found out to their cost when they plunged on to a bandwagon, whether science fiction or sociological analysis, which appeared alien to their previous record. Remember the publisher does not sell to the public, but to the bookselling trade: indeed he is discouraged from doing anything else by the Booksellers' Association. If the trade cannot be persuaded that the publisher had a potential best-seller, they will not stock it and the public will not find it in the shops. Only an 'underground' best-seller will work, and then slowly, without massive piles of the book in bookshops and generous window displays.

The first move in launching a book is for the publisher to write a blurb. This should not be written by the latest acquisition from Newnham College but by the publisher himself, perhaps *à deux* with a colleague over too much sherry, to achieve that special flavour of what the Americans call 'boss copy'. The blurb, or poop-sheet, or *bla-bla* (as the French say) is a delicate instrument which must not be distorted if it is to be useful. It has three purposes; to convince the bookselling trade that the book is worthwhile; to convince the reviewer that the book is worth reviewing and to convince the man in the book shop, who has by then, perhaps, vaguely heard of it, to buy it after he has picked it up. The triple-purpose blurb is difficult to write and many publishers take the trouble to prepare a special information sheet for the trade and indeed to regard the catalogue as a vehicle for trade publicity and not for the general public. Doubleday, for instance, advertising the new Taylor Caldwell, *Testimony of Two Men*, came out quite brassily with: 'This big, long, dramatic novel has a triple-barrelled appeal, first it is written by Taylor Caldwell, one of America's best-selling authors, second it is about a doctor and, third, the "Rebecca" theme has been cleverly woven into the story, giving the book fascinating overtones of the Gothick novel.' And in the catalogue the plot of *Testimony of Two Men* is summarized in a further three lines. So in one short paragraph they convey to the trade the reminder that Taylor Caldwell has previously sold; they make the point that the book concerns a doctor, and doctors have never yet failed; they make a neat analogy with *Rebecca*, Daphne du Maurier's immortal (a word one should never use) best-seller, and they even get on to the current fashion in America for the Gothick. This blurb on the jacket flap would certainly antagonize the reviewers but, of course, it is not meant for them.

Publishers' blurbs have developed their own form of code clichés; all are to be avoided. Here are some of them:

*Kafkaesque* means obscure

*Saga* means too long (the editor suggested cuts but the author was adamant)

*Frank* or *outspoken* means obscene
*Well-known* means unknown
*Rebellious* means the author uses bad language
*Savage* means the author revels in sadism
*Ingenious* usually means unbelievable
*Sensitive* means homosexual

The blurb writer is also prone to compare his offering with established writers. Favourites, besides Kafka, are Conrad, J. D. Salinger and Beckett. He will also put in clues for the bookseller: like 'major', which means, 'We promise to advertise.'

Apart from a description of the book, usually on the inside flap of the book jacket, there will be, on the inside back flap, a *curriculum vitae* or 'bio.' of the author, and possibly a photograph. Most authors like having early photographs of themselves on their books, but unless they are pretty or very peculiar-looking this self-indulgence should be discouraged. Quotes from reviewers of the author's previous works usually please the author. These too should be used with restraint. It is better to reprint in full one perceptive – another awful word – review than have a series of jerky comments like: 'Marvellous' – *Daily Mail*, 'Brilliant' – *Daily Express*, 'Unusual' – *Sunday Times*, 'Worthy to rank with *Gone with the Wind*' – *Rochdale Observer*, and so on. If an author has previously written one absolute blockbuster, it is the sad but invariable practice of publishers to print its title in bold type on the jacket: it's impossible to find a book by Harold Robbins without a reference, in enormous type, to his authorship of *The Carpetbaggers*. This simple trick usually works.

Simultaneous with the blurb-writing there will be the 'talk-up stage'. Publishers have been accused not of publishing but of 'privishing', i.e. of hugging a title to their bosoms and not trumpeting it abroad. This is true, but only because they are too poor to buy time or space in the media of mass communication. In fact, publishers are the most loquacious, indiscreet and boastful tribe when the egg has just been hatched (although, like the egg, they tend to cool off).

Sometimes luck is on their side. Messrs William Collins

achieved their million-pound turnover that glorious month because they published at the same time *Doctor Zhivago* and Field-
Marshal Montgomery's memoirs, and both became news stories:
Pasternak refused the Nobel Prize and Montgomery refused to
admit that Eisenhower had the qualities of a general. It is very
hard for a publisher to create such controversies, even with the
assistance of the beadiest Fleet Street press agent; what he can do
is lobby, as quickly as possible, the television and radio programmes to try to ensure that his author is talked about beyond
the salons of SW3 and out into the factories, pubs and working
men's clubs of the North. It was reported of *The Carpetbaggers*
that seven men were each chipping in five bob (as 25p was then
called) to buy a copy.

Let us imagine that Messrs Rosencrantz and Guildenstern have
acquired the rights to translate and publish a scandalous novel
written by the French-born wife of an English Duke.* She is
young and pretty so we start off well: a Duchess plus scandal and
beauty. The book is tolerably well written and is thought to be
extremely indiscreet, a *roman à clef* in fact, say the French publishers, who claim from their offices in the rue du Cherche-
Publicité, Paris, to have detected clear caricatures of many
politicians and notables on the London scene. The book is un-
agented, and Messrs Rosencrantz and Guildenstern, who can read
French almost as well as Rumanian, have sold it for seven thousand
dollars to an American publisher staying at the Connaught Hotel;
he had been there for three days without buying a book, and was
beginning to feel that he didn't exist. The book gave him a talking
point at cocktail parties – and indeed Rosencrantz and Guildenstern have made quite certain that it is going to be a staple for
some time in such places.

Soon enough, Messrs Rosencrantz and Guildenstern will receive
a telephone call from Whitefriar, a trade columnist whose identity
has been a badly kept secret for many years. They are on their
way. This column is the Hickey of the book trade: no one admits

* The following parody is less improbable than it may seem – witness the successful
promotion of Gaia Servadio's novel *Melinda* (Weidenfeld & Nicolson, London, 1968).

to reading it, everybody quotes it. Whitefriar doesn't disappoint: he promises 'a copper-bottomed best-seller', 'booksellers' tills ringing like Bow Bells', and claims there is a bigger market for this novel than *Coronet Among the Weeds*.

Meanwhile, the Duchess has taken an unwonted 'commercial' flight over to Paris (she usually flies her own plane) where she meets a stringer for the *Evening Standard*; over several Martinis at the Crillon, he declares she has the grace and stalking power of a Black Panther, concealed by the playfulness of a Siamese kitten, etc., etc. At this point a lady scout from Metro-Goldwyn-Mayer's London office asks if she can Xerox a copy and send it over to the States. Rosencrantz and Guildenstern point out quietly that the manuscript is in French and suggest that M.G.M. wait until a proof copy is available. Similar calls come from similar film companies. More interesting, and more to the point, Pan Books send in a letter, only a day or two after several telephone calls from Corgi, Panther, New English Library and Mayflower. Penguin, possibly because they have 232 unpublished novels in their larder, are silent.

A couple of chapters from *Marie, Marie, Marie* (the title was easy to choose; it is international and it sings, said Rosencrantz to Guildenstern) are translated from the French. The pace hots up. *Harper & Queen* offers seventy-five pounds for a chapter and the *Evening Standard* offers five hundred pounds for serial rights. They are accepted. The stage is set. Full-page advertisements have been appearing in both *Smith's Trade News* and the *Bookseller*. The jacket is out three months before publication and the Duchess is known to the public anyway; its success seems assured. There remain only the little matters of garnering all possible free publicity and, of course, getting the right reviews.

There are many TV and radio programmes into which books can be profitably jockeyed, and if the right sort of sights and sounds emerge from the right sort of programme, the effect on sales can be immediate. The 'Today' programme, 'The World at One', 'Late Night Line Up' and even 'Panorama' are receptive to book ideas if they are topical, significant or amusing, and can greatly help sales. (These exposures are best engineered by a specialist in the field – usually a restaurant. Bright-eyed, part-time divorcées are good at this sort of thing.) However, the hardback book buyer belongs to what used to be called the 'carriage trade', which shops at Harrods rather than the British Home Stores, so it is useless to hope for a wide response to the presence of an author or the mention of a book by David Frost or a big story in the *Daily Mirror* – better a column in the *New Statesman* any day! Ten years ago, when that embarrassing and successful programme 'This is Your Life' commanded an alleged audience of twelve million people, the subject one week was a Czech pilot: he had been shot down during the war and blinded, and one of his air crew had offered him his eye. The television company had gone to the trouble to fly in from the then remote and now beleaguered Czechoslovakia his school teacher, his mother, his childhood sweetheart, the member of the air crew who had made the noble gesture and members of his bombing crew. Everyone on stage was in floods of tears, as possibly were the twelve million viewers. The book★ was even held up in the hands of the inimitable Eamonn Andrews. Roughly twelve copies were sold as a result of this display: it was an order from a Co-operative Wholesale Society shop in Ilford, near the author's home.

Messrs Rosencrantz and Guildenstern will be delighted if the Duchess is indiscreet on television, if she is denounced by a back-woods peer as a traitress to her class, if the Bishop of Southwark espouses her cause and if the librarian at Bury, Lancs., refuses to have her book on his sacred shelves. If the class war can be rubbed up to rage around her pretty head, so much the better. However, Messrs Rosencrantz and Guildenstern should hesitate to give a party for the book. Reviewers and literary editors tend to get drunk, leave their copy in a taxi and, the next morning, full of guilt, piously resolve never to mention the book lest they be accused of corruption. Parties do work in the provinces, although publishers should be cautious about entertaining in Scotland where

★ Jo Capka, D.F.C., *Red Sky at Night* (Anthony Blond, London, 1958).

it is traditional for booksellers and librarians, on evenings out, to
be accompanied by their relations.

As for reviews, Messrs Rosencrantz and Guildenstern have to
restrain the Duchess from putting pressure on her friends, the
Press Lords. (N.B. Literary editors don't mind their elbows being
jogged from below, but resent a thunderbolt from above.) The
national daily and weekly press all carry book reviews, and they
'pull' in roughly this order: the *Sunday Times*, the *Observer*, the
*Sunday Telegraph*, the *Financial Times*, the *Sunday Express*, *The
Times*, the *Daily Telegraph*, the *Guardian*, the *Daily Express*, the
*New Statesman*, *The Times Literary Supplement*, the *Listener*, the
*Spectator*, *New Society*, *Tribune*. And then there are provincial
papers like the *Yorkshire Post*, the *Oxford Mail*, the *Sheffield Daily
Telegraph* and the *Western Daily News*, not forgetting the *Bolton
Evening News*, on which Sir Philip Gibbs was once a reporter.
Glossy magazines often feature books both in reviews and as
gossip. A publisher must reckon on sending out between sixty and
a hundred review copies of the most modest novel.

The reviewing establishment has been criticized as being
cliquey, narrow-minded, prejudiced in favour of Oxford and
Cambridge, and out of touch with popular taste: it may be all
those things; it is also fair and totally incorruptible. The journals
they write for in no way reflect the prejudices of their proprietors
and indeed the *Financial Times*, which is one of the many belong-
ings of Lord Cowdray, is a hot-house of left-wing intellectuals,
some of whom are occasionally unleashed on the book pages.
They are also remote from the influence of the paper's advertising
manager, which is just as well because only the bigger firms can
afford a four-inch double column in say, the *Sunday Times* at
£160 unless, like Victor Gollancz with the *Observer*, they con-
cluded a special deal in the 1930s. (That house, incidentally, follows a house style and produces highly distinctive advertising
copy and layout.)

About one hundred books are published every working day in
England, and these are divided by the bookseller into forty-four
separate categories, ranging from 'aeronautics' to 'wireless and

television': naturally, only some of these categories interest the literary editor and the most dominant is 'fiction'. About one novel is published every twenty minutes but the literary pages of the posh Sundays, for instance, are strangely similar in the novels they select to review. This is probably because each literary editor feels that he must represent, in his reviews, all that is going of the best that week and the unlucky reviewer is given fifteen or twenty guineas, nine or ten books, and told to review at least five of them. (A big novel is often handed out to a bigger gun.) The reviewer may not have time to digest each book thoroughly unless he or she is new to the game, and will, of course, rely heavily on the publisher's blurb, which he or she may be tempted to criticize. It is a pity that literary papers, with the limited space available for book reviews (the book review pages are often full of ads, from airlines to distilleries), are not bold enough to select one novel, deal with it in a certain amount of depth and simply list the others worth mentioning. No journal in England, except those almost specialist organs *Encounter*, the *New Left Review*, the *Month*, the *London Magazine* or *The Times Literary Supplement*, has the space to review a book in detail. Perhaps the most profound reviews in the English language are published by the *New York Review of Books* which takes a great deal of time, trouble and type-area over each book it finds worthy, and gives to English critics space they cannot find locally.

The late Simon Marks used to refuse to advertise on the grounds that 'My advertisements are my shop windows,' and a publisher might take the same view of his list. Certainly literary editors are guided in their choice of book for review by the quality of the publishing house which has uttered the volume. They are imprint-conscious, and will respect a publisher who is obviously trying to put out literature as opposed to popular fiction; but in the choice of books to review they will probably be ahead of or more refined than the majority of their readers, arguing that a popular best-seller will always find its public and that, if the publishers don't like it, well then, like Liberace they can cry all the way to the bank.

Not only do reviewers review the same books, they tend to do so in the same way. There is a disturbing similarity of approach among the 'posh' Sundays, for instance, and not one reviewer has the oracular appeal and authority of, say, Arnold Bennett before the war, or Ken Tynan when he reviewed plays for the *Evening Standard* and the *Observer*. However, the wise publisher keeps his mouth shut about these defects when lunching a literary editor, and waits for that distinguished person to say to him over the coffee, 'Well, are you doing anything interesting?'

The literary world is a small one, and literary editors are obviously more susceptible to a novel by a writer whom they have heard about from someone they trust than to, say, a translation. In fact here lies a major weakness of literary London: it is not sufficiently aware of the value of foreign books.

Every year the publishers of practically every country in the world gather at the Frankfurt Book Fair, and fine words are spoken about the international brotherhood of the pen. But in fact literature is not international at all. The stands at Frankfurt bulge with hopeful titles, but with the exception of a few English and American books they are unlikely to be seen again outside their native lands. From an international publishing point of view, Europeans suffer because so many different languages are spoken on the Continent, and of course the smaller the country the worse its lot. English, on the other hand, is the second language in European schools – happily for English and American publishers, who maintain or share representatives to place their books in shops from Madrid to Helsinki.* Where in the British Isles, apart perhaps from Bauermeister's in Edinburgh, would you find a best-selling German or Dutch novel? The export market of European publishers is confined to the sale of translation rights, which are handled by a few key figures in Paris, London, Milan and New York, and these sales are pitifully few.

British and American publishers will rarely buy translation rights without working in concert and planning to share the costs, and the problems. First of all, there is the difficulty of assessing

---

* It is unlikely, whatever President Pompidou's aspirations may be, that French books will ever sell as well in England as English books sell in France.

E

foreign writers. The brilliant Polish writer Witold Gombrowicz had to wait many years before appearing in English, and in his case it was only because he was first translated into French that his works appeared as quickly as they did.* It took James Joyce years to convince Putnam's that Italo Svevo, a Jew writing in a Triestino Italian dialect, was a genius.† Then there is the difficulty of finding a good translator, and the additional expense of translation fees. And the publisher must also calculate the possible time and trouble expended on gaining the author's approval of the translation. Publishers like Secker & Warburg, with their Japanese list, and John Calder, with his French list, have been brave in introducing foreign talent to the Anglo-American market. But one can count on the fingers of one hand the foreign writers who have been successfully translated into English since the war.

There are very few permanent liaisons between Continental and Anglo-American firms; perhaps the most famous is the link through the late Manya Harari of the Harvill Press, who brought *Doctor Zhivago* and *The Leopard* to Messrs Collins from the Italian communist publisher Feltrinelli. The selling prestige of American and British best-sellers has meant that they have dominated the world market in translation. From *Gone with the Wind* by Margaret Mitchell, *The Carpetbaggers* by Harold Robbins, to *The Naked Ape* by Desmond Morris (translated into twenty-four languages), comfortable pickings have been earned by British and American authors, but the traffic the other way is sparse.

British publishers complain that the apathy of reviewers discourages them in their costly attempts to introduce the best (as they think) of contemporary foreign literature to the English market. One would have expected literary editors to realize that the very fact that a book has been selected to appear in translation bespeaks an excellence beyond the normal run of home-produced novels. But no, alas; only the big guns get noticed, and then only

---

* *Pornografia*, tr. A. Hamilton (Calder, London, 1966).
† His two books, *Confessions of Zeno* and *A Man Grows Older*, were reissued in Britain by Secker & Warburg in 1962 and are now in Penguin.

when they totter across the Channel trailing clouds of glory from some gigantic foreign literary prize.

Publishing is perhaps the most investigated trade in Great Britain, but no one has yet discovered a means of working out why a book sold well or badly. The value of advertising, word-of-mouth recommendation, short good reviews versus long bad ones, is constantly speculated upon. It depends, of course, on the book, but this does not help too much. Let us take two books at different ends of the spectrum. Tom Matthews, the original editor of *Time* Magazine, wrote his autobiography, *Names and Addresses*. It was the subject of enormous reviews in the quality Sundays, and in the tabloids, too, because there were some juicy anecdotes about the tycoon Henry Luce. It was also eminently a reviewers' book, since what reviewer has not yearned to be an editor? It did not sell. *The Godfather*, by Mario Puzo, was hardly reviewed at all but became gradually a phenomenal best-seller on both sides of the Atlantic. Clearly it was through people picking up the book, getting excited, talking about it, ringing up their friends. Bill Targ, the editor-begetter of Putnam's New York, who believed in this title, was asked if he realized he had such a strong book on his hands when he first published it. He replied, 'I knew it was good, but I didn't believe it could be *that* good.'

# 6

## The Economics of Publishing

The economics of the trade or general publisher differ from any
other manufacturer in that his raw material is not so much the
bland product of the automated paper mill but the complicated
efforts of the human mind. When a publisher says that the best
authors are dead authors, he means that the latter cannot torment
him by being late with their manuscripts, demanding more money,
threatening to go off to another publisher, or telephoning him in
the middle of the night. From the financial point of view, the best
authors of all are the long dead – those whose works are out of
copyright.

There are at least six editions of *David Copperfield*, all selling
steadily, and when someone has the idea of reprinting a classic,
like the original Mrs Beeton, or an 1893 Sears Roebuck catalogue,
the cost of reproduction is gloriously free from fees.

But if a publisher is to concern himself with the output of living
authors, and without this in mind he might as well be a monu-
mental mason, he must approach his profession with equal
amounts of charm and efficiency.

There are no objective rules for the charm contest, but in
publishing it must be held to subsume an autocratic sort of style
of the kind possessed by Mrs Blanche Knopf, Sir Victor Gollancz
and Sir Stanley Unwin, all of whom possessed irritating qualities
which would have got them nowhere in I.B.M. but which
served them well in their very individual pursuit and development
of their own authors. Fewer personalities like these will emerge in

the publishing world (there are still plenty left in the acting profession) and the all-purpose company man, with an understanding of conglomerate politics, will dominate as more and more mergers take place.

But let us turn hurriedly from this consideration and proceed to the neutral area of efficiency, not before saying that it is possible to justify the publication of a ration of difficult and money-losing books in the area, say, of literature or unfashionable politics, on the grounds that to a discerning but influential band of people who care about such things, eccentric effort lends colour and P.R. appeal to a list.

A publisher who goes bankrupt is of no use to God, Mammon or literature. He should not immolate himself, his concern and his backers on the predictable apathy of the public to the visionary and esoteric works of his friends. He should see himself more as a talent-spotter than as a trend-setter, balancing his books and ensuring that, while he can indulge in a little of what he fancies, the bulk of his output should be what the public is able and willing to consume. There is also the question of size – a problem well described by Leonard Woolf in the last volume of his autobiography.* Apropos his dealings over the Hogarth Press with John Lehmann, Woolf proved right, and sheltered happily with Chatto & Windus. Lehmann split with Woolf and the Hogarth Press to found, supported by Purnell the printers, John Lehmann Ltd, which published much literature before going out of business.

A publisher is no different to any other businessman in his pursuit of efficiency: viz, he must watch the ratio of his overheads to his turnover; he must be concerned with cash-flow; with the amount of times his stock turns over in a year; with the efficiency of his sales organization; with the amount of money he has out to authors in advances, particularly overseas; with the off-loading

* *The Journey Not the Arrival Matters* (Hogarth Press, London, 1969). Here Leonard Woolf snipes back at John Lehmann, who implied in *his* autobiography that he had built up the Hogarth Press himself. The two parted allegedly on the issue of expansion, Lehmann being for and Woolf gloomily against. The latter maintained that there were two possible ways of publishing, one large-scale and one very small; that the first led to misery and loss of control, and the second allowed for self-expression and happiness. In one way he is right; a small business can break all the rules.

and sale of the paperback, book club, American, European and film rights, etc. and with the economic costing of his products. We shall end this chapter with an analysis of two case histories of Blond publications – publishers are rather coy about revealing such figures so one is forced back on to examples that are to hand – but let's first break down some of the big items that will appear in any business's balance sheet.

*Overheads.* These tend to be high in general publishing because of the cost of charm – a Bloomsbury house rather than a cubic space in a post-war office block, the odd chandelier and debutante dancing around, lengthy (though profitable) lunches. All this enjoyable frippery can end up as a figure of 45 to 50 per cent in the costing of a book. In educational publishing, where authors are less susceptible and where the mark-up is lower, $3\frac{1}{2}$ to 4 times as opposed to 5 to 6 times, the overheads are appropriately and proportionately lower.

*Cash-flow.* In publishing this should be more properly described as a cash-*ebb* and certainly here, as in the variety of products he produces, the publisher is trying to gain profits against the current business tide; in order to produce a book he may have to lay out hundreds of pounds to an author, wait one, two or even three years before the book is produced, four to six months before it is published and another month or so before he can recoup any revenue therefrom, save through the sale of rights, or sheets,* of which more below. Thus publishers, unless they are very nippy, have to be highly capitalized. There is no rule of thumb, but fifty pence in the pound of turnover has been suggested as a medium figure. Quite prosperous publishers have been caught between

* The sale of sheets, or a 'sheet deal' deserves explanation. It means that the British publisher can sell to another (invariably American) publisher copies of his own edition, printed simultaneously, with the American's imprint. Fredric Warburg in his book on publishing *An Occupation for Gentlemen* describes how, before the war, the directors of Routledge & Kegan Paul would anxiously lay out their wares on the table for the visiting American publisher to sample and order from. Nowadays, the invention of photolithography has meant that British and American publishers only need 'camera' copies of each other's books. Both these processes explain the prevalence in each other's lists of English and American authors, which constitutes a simple, lively, transatlantic two-way traffic.

high interest rates on one hand and a shortening of credit terms from paper merchants and printers on the other, and have run dry of cash. A publisher in this position either sells out, merges, or slows down his publishing and investment; if he suddenly slows to a halt he will indeed be flooded with cash, but in the same way as a speedboat, stopping suddenly, is flooded by its own wash.

*Stock.* A publisher is the only man qualified to value his own stock, and his view is accepted by accountants unless circumstances – usually unfortunate – force an investigation. The publisher may not be dishonest, simply optimistic, if he over values to reassure himself or his backers, but either way an accountant is lost in the subtleties and oddities of this crucial area of publishing – crucial because with a publisher turning over, say, a hundred thousand pounds, his stock may have a genuine value of fifty thousand.

Stock should be written down annually by a director, on the basis of whichever is the *lower*, the cost of the books or their net realizable value. He arrives at this through a variety of computations, some of them instinctive. It is, for instance, hard to persuade an accountant that a novel published two months ago should be written down from £2·50 to its lowest level, whereas one published three years ago could be kept in at cost since it is selling a steady thousand or so copies a year. It is even possible, although unlikely, that in the case of a high-priced or an often-reprinted college textbook, the stock value could be written *up* as the retail price has been increased. At any rate, the less there is of that, the better.

It is almost impossible for a publisher to estimate exactly the extent of his first print order on a book. Usually through over-optimism and a false equation, which leads him to suppose that the higher the print number and cheaper the unit cost therefore the greater the profit, a publisher will overprint; hence there are always more remainders than books out of stock. A wise publisher will put a remainder value on stock of a novel which has ceased to sell three months after publication. The remainder trade is as old as publishing, and since hardbound books are difficult to destroy,* there's many a bargain at 10p. Incidentally, paperbacks can be remaindered for less than 1p, but are usually pulped.

Of course stock is the physical end product of a mental equation – more often a war – between a book's individual retail selling price in the shops and its economic print run as discussed within the publishing house. This war can often take on a moral flavour. For instance, supposing a publisher decides to take a long foreign translation of a significant novel, and his production manager shows him that he can print 2,000 if the price is £3·50, or 4,000 if the price is £2·50. The argument would be between the cautious who maintain that of such a significant book it should be possible to sell 1,700 or so at £3·50 because 'the libraries will have to have it'; and the other view that the book is so interesting that it's import-ant to give the public the opportunity of buying it. Such argu-ments are never happily resolved and vary from house to house. On the whole, most London houses take the cautious view, with Messrs Cape and Collins as interesting, gutsy exceptions.

It has been said that if the guess of the print number is exactly right, there is something wrong with the book. There are thou-sands of mementos of publishers' optimism in this area in the form of remainders where the cut has been savage. A £2 book will be sold to the trade for as little as 10p and to the public for around 25p. It is possible to make money at this end, witness the rise to fortune of Paul Hamlyn; which brings us to the next item – sales.

*Sales.* Just as Paul Hamlyn, starting allegedly with £500 and a barrow, made a fortune out of the books that publishers couldn't sell, some sales forces in some publishing houses are so inefficient they can't even sell books which are saleable. The problems of selling hardbound books to customers through the bookshops are discussed elsewhere, but here let us remind our-selves that the best the most conventional hardbound publisher can hope for is not to lose too much money from the sales of his

---

* Mr Richard Booth of Hay-on-Wye, who owns more books than any individual in the world, is the source for this: he has tried. He also points out that more books have been published in the last twenty years than in the whole history of mankind; so the problem does not abate.

books. Where then are his profits? They come from subsidiary rights and co-productions.

The sale of rights to book clubs, paperback houses, foreign and American publishers, film companies and newspapers offer the general publisher his only sure source of profit. Novels whose hardbound sales break even with difficulty are expected to recoup in these areas and some publishers have been ingenious enough to sell rights to books without ever having to print them. This neat evasive manœuvre is not uncommonly practised when a publisher who has acquired all rights in a property, and given an advance to an author against revenue from these rights, finds himself too embarrassed, for one reason or another, to publish the thing himself. It's most tactful here to describe the case of *The Consort*, commissioned by the author (as publisher) from Anthony Heckstall-Smith. When the book was read for libel the publisher was warned that publication might provoke riots! It was a lighthearted skit about an imaginary prince consort who goes off on a state visit to a sunlit tropical island and refuses to return. The non-appearance of the book provoked the popular press to run stories about its apparent similarity to some unknown intentions of H.R.H. The Duke of Edinburgh and the publisher was seriously counselled that its publication might imprison him. So, the book was sold for paperback in England, hard and soft back rights in America, film option, a modest Dutch serial and some heavy coverage in that eager consumer of royal nonsense *France Dimanche*. The American publisher plastered the book in towns about to be visited by H.R.H. on his American tour, the book sold quite well, the author got his money, everyone was pleased, and the Prince was reported to be more amused than irritated.

Much more common, and broadcast as little as possible, is the publisher's practice of selling the paperback rights of novels for more than they paid as an advance to the author. The author does not suffer, of course, since he gets 50 per cent of such paperback advances, but it tends to nark agents when a publisher buys the hardback rights for, say, £250 and by the time the contract has been drawn up has already sold the paperback rights for £1,000.

There is one, financially glamorous, exception to the rule that generally publishers do not make money out of book sales and that is in the international world of co-productions, where publishers like Paul Hamlyn, George Rainbird, the late Walter Neurath of Thames and Hudson and above all Wolf Foges of Aldus Books, the father of them all and the quondam employer of the last two, have made fortunes and even a little fame. The product is known dolefully to publishers not in this complex and multi-lingual business as the non-book. The principle is that an innocuous, illustratable subject – Great Rivers, or Canaletto – be taken, printed in the cheapest country and sold to the more expensive: thus the book might originate in Yugoslavia, Bilbao or Hong Kong and be sold through established links literally all over the world in a series of 'sheet' deals.

Devaluation in the U.K., the high cost of composing or setting in the United States and the increasing competence and salesmanship of British printers has meant that high-priced books can often be sold to America with an advance and a sheet order. If he does his sums right the British publisher should be home and dry with his American order and have his own edition to sell as a present.

Let us now take three case histories which emphasize to the point of exaggeration the difference between general and textbook or school book publishing:*

THE GURU AND THE GOLF CLUB by David Benedictus
David Benedictus's first novel, published when he was twenty-three, was called *The Fourth of June* and was a funny, savage attack on Eton College, which delighted most reviewers and yielded anonymous letters from elderly chaps in Clubs. It was made into a play, nearly into a film, and the publication rights were sold all over the world. His second, *You're A Big Boy Now*, was unkindly reviewed, didn't sell, but a film was made of it and the publishers were still happy. His third, *Hump*, was a curious, indigestible novel about a clown with this unfortunate deformity, which is gradu-

---

* The author is grateful to Mr David Benedictus, Miss Gillian Freeman and Mr Peter Moss for their public spiritedness in allowing these figures to be reproduced.

ally removed from him by a sort of bacon slicer. It didn't sell. His next novel, which we are to analyse, was published in the light of the previous failure and the publisher decided to print the modest number of 2,750. (Please, gentle reader, don't be shocked; quite a lot of authors you have heard of are printed now in runs of 1,800.) The following table is the publisher's I.B.B. (Individual Book Balance); to it should be added revenue of £250 (which is 50 per cent of the £500 advance) from a paperback sale and, of course, always the *possibility* that somebody, somewhere, some day may want to make a film or a translation. General publishers have often had their hopes in the most unlikely properties justified years later. This kind of expectation does not apply to the ordinary school book.

---

COST ANALYSIS – THE GURU AND THE GOLF CLUB

1 printing – 2,750

PUBLISHED @ £1·50 – 2,750 copies

---

|  |  | % on Gross Sales |  |  |
|---|---|---|---|---|
| TOTAL COST b/fwd. | 1,156 |  | 2,750 | Edition |
| (per copy) |  |  | – | Gratis |
| GROSS PROFIT c/d. | 1,164 | 50.1% GP | 430 | free @ 75p |
|  |  |  | 2,309 | Sales @ £1·50 |
|  | 2,320 |  | Less Discount $33\frac{1}{3}\%$–40% |  |
| Less o/heads @ 45% of t/o | 1,044 |  |  | 2,320 t/o |
|  |  |  | GROSS PROFIT b/d 1,164 |  |
| NET PROFIT | 120 |  |  |  |

BREAKEVEN ON Approx. 1,200 Sales   5·2% net profit on t/o

10·3% profit on investment

---

The modest tale told in these simple figures shows the scale of the average mildly successful novel. No wonder Wall Street is not impressed by general publishers. Let's try another.

THE ALABASTER EGG by Gillian Freeman
This English writer had six novels to her credit when *The
Alabaster Egg* was published in the autumn of 1970. Her first,
*The Liberty Man*, had been sold to Mark Longman by the author
of this book when a literary agent, and she came under the Blond
imprint with a pseudonymous novel ('Eliot George') called *The
Leather Boys*, which was profitably converted to the screen.
Indeed her cinematic qualities are appreciated in Hollywood
where she can earn $30,000 writing a film script more easily than
in penning a novel – to reinforce our point about authors'
earnings.

*The Alabaster Egg* was a pretty-looking book about mad
Ludwig of Bavaria and, as a contrapuntal theme, the diary of a
middle-aged Jewish refugee living in Hampstead, was ambitiously
woven in.

---

INDIVIDUAL BOOK BALANCE as at
February 24th, 1971

*Title:* ALABASTER EGG
*Published:* October 12th, 1970
*Price:* £1·50
*Print No.:* 3,110 copies
*Bind No.:* 3,110 copies

|  |  |  |  |
|---|---|---|---|
| *Revenue:* | | | |
| Trade Sales – Home Sales: 1,214 copies | | | £1,195 |
| Export Sales: 430 copies | | | £ 328 |
| *Rights* | – | – | |
| | | | £1,523 |
| Less Production Cost: | £1,504 | | |
| Authors' advances less Royalties earned | 619 | | (£2,123) |
| | Profit (Loss) | | (£ 600) |
| | + Stock 1,468 copies bound | | £ 746 |
| | | | £ 146 |
| Less overheads: | 50% on turnover | | (£ 761) |
| | Profit (*Loss*) | | (£ 615) |

It was approvingly noticed, since Miss Freeman has a reputation, by almost every organ of opinion, from the BBC Overseas Service broadcasts to the *Financial Times*, but the above figures tell clearly and sadly why publishers will not for very long be able to afford literature. It is further significant that if this novel had been published three years before, the paperback rights would certainly have been sold.

By contrast, let us take a more than usually successful textbook, *History Alive*. It started off with volume 4 – the last book in the course – for the simple reason that teachers had expressed a need for this particular volume. It was a history book, on a lower level

---

INDIVIDUAL BOOK BALANCE as at: 31st December, 1970

*Title:* HISTORY ALIVE Book 4

| | | |
|---|---|---|
| *Published:* 30/6/67 | *Reprints:* | 10,000 1967 |
| | | 10,000 1968 |
| *Price:* 67½ p | | 10,000 1969 (January) |
| | | 10,000 1969 (December) |
| *Print No:* 50,764 copies | | 15,000 1970 (on order) |
| *Bind No:* 45,471 copies | | |

*Revenue:*

| | | |
|---|---|---|
| *Trade Sales:* | Home 30,501 copies £15,276 | |
| *Export Sales:* | 3,604 copies £1,684 | |
| *Special Sales:* | – | |
| *Rights:** | – | |
| *Less Production Cost:* | £8,083 | £16,960 |
| *Less Royalties:* | £1,417 | (£ 9,500) |
| | Profit (Loss) | £7,460 |
| + Stock | Bound 11,366 copies £1,704 | |
| | Sheets 5,293 copies £374 | |
| | | £9,538 |
| Less overheads 45% on turnover: | | (£7,632) |
| | Profit (Loss) | £1,906 |

\* School book publishing is essentially national, and rights are rare.

---

than was already available, describing the history of the last fifty years for secondary modern and comprehensive school children between the ages of 12–16. The publishers embroidered the lively narrative with what were really strip cartoons; these described key themes, like the rise of Hitler, in comic drawings which, it was hoped, it would be a pleasure to learn from. As we can see from its printing history, the idea worked. The book has splendid prospects, as have Books 3, 2, 1 and an introductory book in the same series. The author, Peter Moss, can look forward to a steady income from this course for the next ten or fifteen years. (Incidentally, it was printed in East Germany, which would have prevented it from being imported into the United States of America.)

Note the number of copies printed, the high stock, the confident fifth reprint, the much higher net profit on turnover and the much higher profit on investment and you will understand why successful textbook publishing can be successful business, and how difficult it is to succeed in the other, lighter, glossier, area.

In order to launch *The Guru and the Golf Club* the publishers asked a couple of gurus to lunch at a golf club, and the event was widely reported. For the launch of *History Alive* Book 4 there was no such junketing but there was a solid, persistent mailing to all history teachers. There you are.

Note too that the contribution to overheads of *History Alive* Book 4 (one, incidentally, in a series of now six books), has, at the date of that individual book balance, produced £7,632 for the publisher. (Clearly this is a falsely high overhead but it does pay the salary of a junior editor for five years! So far publishers have not come up with an adjustable overhead which would decline as the book progressed.)

Profitability in publishing, as in any other business, depends on establishing the right relationship between turnover and overheads. Overheads have mounted to the point where costing the book will include 50 per cent or more for this item, slightly less for a textbook, and the reason for the sudden jump in book prices in the early 'seventies is that the cost of print production, taking 1966 as a base of 100, has risen 36 in three years. Publishers are always psychologically reluctant to price up books, and the reason for many failures since the war has been the under-pricing of books.

*Size*. The specification of a new motor car will show the maximum speeds desirable in each gear and also the petrol consumption at the most economic speed in top gear. There are so many publishers, so many products and so little money in the whole operation that it is difficult to generalize, so let's pursue this dangerous analogy in terms of gears as amount of turnover. Starting with:

First Gear. Here the operation will be one man and a girl and the turnover up to £40,000 per annum. Sales will be contracted out to another publisher and if there is a packer it will be the publisher's own father. (Ernest Hecht of Souvenir Press Ltd, probably the most perennially profitable firm in London, started in this way.) The publisher in first gear might do anything from one book to Leonard Woolf's fifteen books a year, and could be extremely profitable simply because, having very few overheads, his gross profits will so nearly approximate to his net. Incidentally, one of the most successful publishers in England, Ross McWhirter, essentially publishes *one* book, *The Guinness Book of Records*, and owns one printing press for this purpose.

Second Gear. £40,000–£120,000 per annum. This is an awkward change up. The publisher in first gear will have acquired too many books to be able to manage without an editor or partner, he will be dissatisfied with his sales arrangements, he will be flexing his muscles and will have moved out of his back room into offices of his own. Get out of this gear as soon as you can into:

Third Gear. £120,000–£300,000 per annum. More books, possibly up to forty a year, more editors, more salesmen, the odd best-seller, the odd rights 'coup', conversations with the city, printers, extended credit, problems – but if he keeps his head there could also be profit.

Fourth Gear – top or overdrive. £300,000–£?M. Here anything

could happen. He could have been staked by a bank, could have amalgamated with another publisher, acquired another imprint. He has become an organization, judged not so much by the books he produces as by the editors he hires to find the books. He may be richer but is constantly boring his young men about the charms of pottering along in first.

In fact, on current form this is probably the sanest gear to stay in. Desmond Elliott of Arlington Books is probably more profitable on his turnover of £30,000 a year than a giant like Macmillan, which has registered losses for three years running. In 1969–70 the British Printing Corporation virtually disbanded its book publishing operations, leading to the unemployment of between ninety and one hundred trained personnel. Similarly Thomson, who has dismembered the general publishing side of the ancient imprint of Nelson and scattered the bits to Hamish Hamilton and Michael Joseph, which they also own. The net decline in public* spending on education and the net decline in book purchasing in the U.K. are the two most powerful factors contributing to this grey scene.

---

\* I.e. ratepayers' money in public libraries and L.E.A. money in school libraries.

# 7

---

## Paperbacks

The story is that the wife of a manager at Woolworth's (Woolworth's managers have always enjoyed more autonomy than their Marks & Spencer colleagues) persuaded her husband to have a go. He'd brought back a sample from the office and she had enjoyed it – a paper-covered, bright-blue book entitled *Ariel* (a life of Shelley by André Maurois) published in 1935 by Allen Lane, price 6d.*

'Paperbacks', or to be more precise paper-bound as opposed to cloth-bound books, were not a totally new idea; there had been Tauchnitz, there had been Albatross, and Hodder & Stoughton had their Yellow Books. But what was new was to put out a famous, popular book, for sixpence. Allen Lane (the nephew of John Lane of The Bodley Head, publisher of, among other classics, *Ulysses*) had of course first approached the booksellers, but they rejected the idea with horror, imagining the total collapse, if these paperbacks were successful, of their hardbound business and no vicarious accretion of book interest worth mentioning. So he tried Woolworth's. The moment the books sold in Woolworth's, the booksellers changed their minds and soon little Penguins in their thousands, orange for fiction, green for detective stories, blue for biography, wended their way around England and across the

---

* On the same day in July nine other Penguins appeared. Note that at least seven are, thirty-six years later, still going strong: Ernest Hemingway, *A Farewell to Arms*; Eric Linklater, *Poets Pub*; Susan Ertz, *Madame Clair*; Dorothy L. Sayers, *The Unpleasantness at the Bellona Club*; Agatha Christie, *Murder at the Links*; Beverley Nichols, *Twenty-Five;* E. H. Young, *William;* Mary Webb, *Gone to Earth*; Compton Mackenzie, *Carnival*.

world. The schoolboy, the unemployed man, the commuter, could all afford sixpence. These were no 'station novels', as the Spanish call pulp literature, they were the best that Allen Lane – no great litterateur but an uncanny connoisseur of what would please, of what would sell – could buy. In the war, Penguin boomed, legitimately, for you could print more works for less money on less paper in Penguin than in any other format, and Penguin's war-time allocation of paper was based on a lucky pre-war bumper order. After a heavy day in the 1940s, checking the sky with the *Air Spotter's Guide* provided by Penguin, thousands of British civilians would relax happily with E. V. Rieu's translation of *The Odyssey*, published by Penguin, whose sales to a new culture-hungry generation would have made even Homer nod happily.

But Penguin titles, and until recently their covers, were never sensational or salacious, and it was clear that the format offered an opportunity for the sale of popular fiction to a less serious and obviously greater section of the nation than Penguins appealed to. It didn't need much imagination to see, Allen Lane having first tilled the ground, that if a popular novel could sell thousands of copies at a guinea, tens of thousands could be sold for two and six. (The respective prices are now more like £1·95 and 30p or even 37½p.)

Between 1945 and the late 1960s there were many new entries into the paperback market, and some heavy losses. Traditionally, British paperback firms are coy about their print and sales figures, and indeed for publicity reasons tend to boast a little wildly about both. Recently Frederick H. Christian (pseudonym for Fred Nolan who has worked for Granada and writes Westerns for Corgi) published in *Books and Bookmen* an analysis of what the market might be. He worked out that there was an annual sale of at least 160 million units and that this was shared, divided roughly as to 60/40 home and export; after consultation we have modified his figures and the breakdown is shown opposite.

Paperback houses would doubtless contend these findings, partly because no audited figures are available and partly because to some houses success depends entirely on the volume of units sold. (It is unlikely that any unattached paperback house with sales of less than ten million units per annum is making a profit, bearing in mind they have no other source of revenue, e.g. from the sale of rights.)

Total likely *sales* market, including
importations, say 125,000,000

| | |
|---|---|
| Penguin | 27 million |
| Pan | 17 million |
| Corgi | 13 million |
| Fontana | 13 million |
| Hodder | 6 million |
| Panther | 5 million |
| Mayflower | 4 million |
| Sphere | 4 million (may be high) |
| N.E.L. | 3 million |
| Imports | 33 million |

Pan began as the paperback end of the same consortium (Macmillan, Collins, Heinemann, Hodder & Stoughton) of British publishers who owned the Reprint Society, steered by the founder Alan Bott, who created the only 'vertical' set-up in publishing. It now belongs to Macmillan and Heinemann alone and is known for shrewd, long sales, middle-brow fiction like Nevil Shute, the occasional non-fiction special and the late Ian Fleming. The curly haired boy-piper Pan – their colophon – is rarely in a tantrum and has been continuously managed by Clarence Paget whose tastes, middle of brow and of age,* are reflected in the solid reputation and sales which Pan enjoy throughout the British Commonwealth. Nothing revolutionary may be expected from this quarter, but should there be a revolution no doubt there would be a Pan Special devoted to it.

The sales of Pan books have undoubtedly suffered from the

* It is relevant and fair to mention that Pan published Alan Sillitoe's *Saturday Night and Sunday Morning*, which inaugurated their Million Copy Silver Trophy Award, subsequently earned three times running by Ian Fleming and then dropped.

demise of Ian Fleming, each of whose Bond stories clocked up a
steady million-plus – Adam Diment's *The Dolly Dolly Spy* is
hardly a chip off that old block – and from the increase of
Fontana, Collins's very own paperbacks, which now occupy
third place with Corgi in unit sales. Fontana is the satrapy of one
of Billy Collins's (q.v.) sons, Mark, and has the first pick of that
mighty house's list.

In 1961, Corgi – wholly owned subsidiary of Bantam Books,
the most successful American paperback company – underwent
a reshuffle of management, at the same time publishing *Lolita* by
Vladimir Nabokov, the sales of which now exceed 800,000. They
are now owned, together with Bantam and American hardcover
publisher Grosset & Dunlap, by National General Film Corporation, one of the largest motion-picture distributors in America,
and have what is probably the strongest backlist of any publisher
save Penguin. The mass-market emphasis of their list is of the
widest possible range, and besides *Lolita* they have sold large
quantities of, among others, *The Scourge of the Swastika* by Lord
Russell of Liverpool, *Valley of the Dolls* by Jacqueline Susann
(both over 800,000), *The Ginger Man* by J. P. Donleavy (750,000),
*The Naked Ape* by Desmond Morris (500,000) and *Catch-22* by
Joseph Heller (500,000). Given the current growth-rate in what
has been for the past two years a difficult period for most paperback publishers, they must soon be in a position to challenge Pan
for second place in the list.

Panther, which was started after the war on their gratuities, by
two erstwhile 'erks', Joe Pacey and Harry Assael, was sold to
Sidney Bernstein's Granada publishing group for over half a
million in 1966. With no publishing experience behind them –
possibly an asset in the paperback field – these two former Air
Force persons knocked a hole in the market with titles like *Camp
on Blood Island* and, with the same appeal but of much higher
quality, *The Naked and the Dead* by Norman Mailer. They are now
under the trendy editorship of William Miller and John Boothe,
known in the trade as Tweedledum and Tweedledee, publishing
enterprising works of literature and often pulling a fast one on

Penguin and on Pelican with 'Sonnie' Metha's imprint Paladin.

New English Library is a subsidiary of New American Library. It was started by Kurt Enoch and Victor Weybright, former Penguin employees in the U.S.A., now comprises Ace Books and Four Square Books and has been notable for dramatic ups and downs in this volatile market. Possibly the biggest post-war up was *The Carpetbaggers*, which sold millions.

Even Lord Thomson had a bit of a setback with his paperback imprint, Sphere, the latest big-timer on the scene; they have published Robert Carrier with some success, and Mr Churchill's life of his ancestor, Marlborough, which, like *The Forsyte Saga* enjoyed the backing of a television series. Sphere's earlier history was shattering, culminating in the disastrous publication of *Only When I Larf* by Len Deighton, for which they paid £27,000, printed 300,000 and sold less than 100,000, perhaps experiencing one of the highest return rates in the business. Sphere are now in safer hands and are building their image afresh. They may yet prove to be the only real challenger to the lower-list publishers.

So much for the big league. We are not here concerned with those so-called paperbacks which are simply versions of hardbacks bound in paper. In modern publishing the name 'paperback' should be given only to those books printed very fast (possibly too fast) on a rotary press and selling for a unit price ranging from 20p at the lowest, 30p regular, to 70p and even 90p. Many old houses, among them O.U.P., Methuen, Allen & Unwin, and Constable with their imported Dover Books, attack the campus market with the more agreeable laminated paperback, feeling that the carriage-trade hardback is no longer a desirable consumer object: probably they are right. What they have all significantly failed to do is establish an author in original paperback form: to the curious layman who wonders why so many novels have to be put out at the outrageous price of £1·95 or more, and cannot understand why they cannot be done at 30p, the answer must be that in this country it has been tried and has never, never worked.★

★ Even the genial Tony Godwin, when fiction editor at Penguin, failed with *Exit Six*, a collection of short stories by James Leo Herlihy of subsequent *Midnight Cowboy* fame.

Successful paperbacks have enormous sales – occasionally a million in England, often two million or more in the U.S.A. This means that when it comes to acquiring, promoting or even inventing a best-selling author, the paperback publisher's purse is so much longer than his hardback confrère's that he can dominate the agent with a big advance. In this way the tail wags the dog. Big guns like Harold Robbins, Irving Wallace and James Michener in the U.S.A. are increasingly controlled by the paperback houses who will shop around for hardback imprints to pre-publish as stalking horses and review-getters only. It is a humiliating role for the hardback publishers, though many of them have been happy to accept it, despite the ukase of the Publishers' Association which has a precise recommended scale for the division of paperback royalties. The strength and eagerness of the paperback market has steadily narrowed the time gap between hard and paperback publication, and in cases like these where the rights are owned by paperback houses, hardback publishers have been obliged, if they wish to retain an author, to conform. There are compensations: the British publishers of Harold Robbins's *The Adventurers* had only six weeks between hardback and paperback publication in the U.K., but nevertheless, such was the strength of this remarkable author, they contrived to sell fourteen thousand copies – and that ain't hay.

It is increasingly difficult for fiction of high literary calibre from rare or unknown authors to succeed in the paperback market, roughly a third of which is controlled directly or indirectly by W. H. Smith and the paperback wholesale house Bookwise. This means that hardback fiction must also find other forms in which to reach the limited public which buys books. A cheap alternative format would be electrically typed Roneos.* But quite apart from this kind of innovation, there must be more liaison between hard and soft publishers who are, after all, in the same business, the difficult business of selling books. And each side needs the other.

But why are there 'sides' at all? Why, hardback publishers are often asked, don't they also run a paperback line? Well, one reason

* There will be experiments in this field designed to appeal to the alienated young.

is that the outlets are as different as Fortnum and Mason is from a local Tesco. Many a London publisher will do more business with Hatchards and Foyle's than with all Messrs W. H. Smith's 300 branches. Paperback houses are competing against each other in a mass market and must employ the appropriate and not always delicate techniques. There are relatively few of them, each punching out between twelve and forty titles a month, panting for display in coffee shops and supermarkets round the world. Without exposure they die; there is no time for them to be 'discovered'. Hence 'loss leaders' are published to create a splash for the imprint. The unsold copies are returned for credit, and these flocks of unwanted homers can be massive. Not only their trade practices but also their personnel make of paperback publishing an intensely competitive and different world. It has often been said that the colourful young Welshman Gareth Powell, once managing director of the New English Library, could never have been a hardback publisher; formerly a truck driver, he emigrated on an assisted* passage to Australia with his Rolls-Royce. All the originality and shove in most paperback firms is directed to sales, whence their only revenue. In this climate, the success of Penguin's is remarkable. They have three thousand titles, mostly unsensational, in print, and still perform better than any other imprint.

If a big book is on offer to London publishers, usually from the United States, and the agent demands a large advance, an auction may occur; this will trigger off a sub-auction among the paperback houses, without which the hardback publisher could not, with his lesser liquidity, finance the purchase. This practice may be unethical, but it enables the hardback publisher to pre-sell his manuscript to a paperback house (n.b. there are many hardback publishers and very few paperback publishers) for sums as high as £25,000 against rising royalties of $7\frac{1}{2}$, 10, $12\frac{1}{2}$ and even 15 per cent which reflect variations in the split from 50/50 to 60/40.

The publisher of general fiction usually makes no profit on his volume sales and must look to subsidiary rights for this bit of his balance sheet. The first natural source is a cheap reprint of his

* Or so the story ran, later disproved.

experimental wares, and sometimes before taking a novel on he will shop round the paperback houses for a commitment. So a first novel which would sell under two thousand copies can be sold for hundreds or even thousands of pounds in the paperback market, and will be published in paperback between eighteen months and two years after the hardback edition. Despite the articulate and often savage protests of authors and their representatives, this bizarre but practical procedure is likely to continue, since without it the publication of new novels in the conventional and costly hardback form will cease.

Speed and bandwagonry, which means alertness to new films, new pop stars, new television programmes and new trends, are much more crucial in the paperback than in the hardback world. Paperback firms can and must produce their books faster (a 35p-paperback novel with a larger than average run – fifty thousand copies – can be printed on a Strachan and Henshaw book rotary press in ten hours) and must 'tie-in' with West End openings and television series, world events like going to the moon or the assassination of an American politician. These urgent themes lend themselves to 'simultaneous' publication, which means that the public is offered two versions of a title on the same day: the hardbound publisher produces an edition at, say, £2 which he will sell mainly to libraries, and the paperback publisher produces an edition at, say, 35p or 40p which he sells to the public on the hoped-for wave of publicity. In cases like this the paperback house has paid for most of the advance, and there may be a saving in joint 'setting' of the type.

I will end this chapter on paperbacks with the saga of *Ulysses* by James Joyce, the twentieth-century classic most harassed by censorship on both sides of the Atlantic. It was eventually published in hardback in England by John Lane, The Bodley Head, and dwells as a symbol of literacy in a mouldy green cover on many shelves. The late Sir Stanley Unwin bought The Bodley Head in 1937 and sold it in 1957 to Max Reinhardt for £75,000. In 1969 Sir Allen Lane bought the paperback rights of *Ulysses* from The Bodley Head for £75,000!

# 8

## Textbooks

The hairiest philistine, whose grown-up reading is the illustrated pages of *Playboy*, must hold as one of his least treasured childhood memories the dour but crucial image of a textbook. Typically the cover would have been green, the type small, the illustrations (if any) meagre and the title (e.g. *First Steps in Correct English*) unenticing.

The creation under the 1944 'Butler' Education Act of secondary modern schools, and their modification later into comprehensive schools, has created a market for textbooks that are brighter in appearance and content; nowadays pupils less amenable than their forefathers to discipline may be lured to learn and even to stay on in school longer than they wish. So a crop of new names like Schonell, Unstead, Ridout, Rowe, Young and Rosby have submerged the hoary figures of Hall and Knight, Oliver and Botting and Mr Pendlebury.

Despite an earnest attempt to give their products a new look, the 'pure' textbook publishers like Blackie, Ginn, Bell and Edward Arnold are still in a world apart from their general or trade confrères. The editors are never at or give the sort of parties which make the *Evening Standard*. They have all the gaiety of owls and the proneness to gossip of Trappists, and are reticent about the amount of money they make for their employers. Collectively they constitute an independent division of the Publishers' Association known as the Educational Publishers' Council. Often ex-schoolmasters, these editors are responsible for the production of thousands of textbooks which are sold in sets of anything from six to a hundred and ninety to the free schools of England.

Textbooks are free to the children in state schools of the United Kingdom and their annual sale at twelve million pounds* in that market out of the total publishing turnover of a hundred and fifty million pounds is not just significant but growing.

Luckily for the young – the first to be brainwashed under authoritarian regimes in other countries – this is a free country and the material which is fed into textbooks by these competitive, intelligent and conscientious editors is, if sometimes dull, free from deliberate propaganda.

There is in British schools (and this always astonishes the layman) no prescription for textbooks other than the required texts which children may have to study for a given examination. For example the East Midlands Board may decide that next year's examination in current literature will include the study of *The Lord of the Flies* (William Golding), *Lucky Jim* (Kingsley Amis) or *Catcher in the Rye* (J. D. Salinger) – yes, they are quite adventurous. Other than these prescribed texts, known as 'set' books, each school in the state system (and we can ignore the public schools which constitute only 5 per cent of the school population) is free to order whatever textbooks from whomsoever they like; the only limitation put upon them is that of money.

This is a real limitation since the 1968–9 figures show that the money spent on school books represented 0·79 per cent of the total on education throughout the land. Compared with other countries like France, Germany or America where the figure is 2 per cent, this is a dispiriting proportion. The national average for 1968–9 was that £1·07 per small head was spent on school books for primary children, and £2·32 for secondary children. Local authorities vary oddly in their largesse. The good burghers of Bournemouth, for instance, possibly the richest town in England, spend only £0·65 per capita on books for primary schools, whereas the children of Gloucestershire are splendidly indulged with £2·39 for primary children and nearly £2·89 for

* A further twelve million pounds is spent on higher educational and technical books.

secondary. Generally speaking, there is no correlation between the wealth of an authority and its expenditure. Belfast, that dreary relic of nineteenth-century industrialism, where unemployment is chronic, is generous, whereas London is relatively mean.

A joint committee of the Association of Education Committees and the National Book League came out with a recommended per capita expenditure, and this is what they suggested:

*Primary textbooks and library books*
| | |
|---|---|
| Good Allowance | £1·325 + £x (for library books) |
| Reasonable Allowance | £1·075 + £x (for library books) |

*Secondary textbooks and library books*
*Under 16 years*
| | |
|---|---|
| Good Allowance | £3·25 |
| Reasonable Allowance | £3 |

*Over 16 years*
| | |
|---|---|
| Good Allowance | £4·875 |
| Reasonable Allowance | £4·5 |

(It seems odd that if they could go to three decimal points in textbooks, they had to be content with an elusive x for library books.)

The state school system in the U.K. is divided into local education authorities, each of which has as its permanent administrative head a chief education officer, subject sometimes to the direction but more often only to the advice of the local education committee. If he is a powerful man he can build schools, commission statues, dismiss, promote, create new educational strata and generally make a nuisance of himself, or, like Sir John Newsom in Hertfordshire, he can become a sort of legend. Sixty per cent of the money for schools comes from the central government – in this area the Ministry of Education has strong persuasive powers – and 40 per cent from the rates – and in this area the chairman of the local education committee can be equally vocal. There are parallel systems of school inspectors; bowler-hatted and umbrella'd

H.M.I.s (Her Majesty's Inspectors), and rather less dauntingly apparelled local inspectors. None of these figures has the power to prescribe books for schools; they can influence, suggest and approve, but they cannot insist that any particular book be ordered.

School books are ordered by headmasters or, in large schools, by heads of departments, paid for by the local authority through one of the (relatively few) educational contractors* and used, of course, by schoolchildren; in other words the people who order them don't pay for them and the people who use them don't order them. A further paradox is that although the money is all from taxes, it is spent on products produced by private enterprise. This could be cited as an excellent example of co-operation in a mixed economy, as I shall now try to explain.

There are 2,830 grammar schools, 600 comprehensive, 4,120 secondary modern and 27,000 primary (infant and junior) schools in the United Kingdom. How are these various and often isolated 'retail outlets' sold books by textbook publishers? And how do the textbook publishers know what to publish? Taking the second point first, the textbook field is a narrow one, and there is great interaction; sales representatives become editors, on retirement Her Majesty's Inspectors join boards of companies, school teachers write books. One publisher has even taught in a school. The annual banquet of the Association of Publishers of Educational Textbooks Representatives (A.P.E.R.) is nearly always addressed by the Minister of Education or his Opposition shadow. Schools may not be visited except by representatives of members of the Educational Publishers' Council and any textbook editor worth his salt will have a wardrobe of friends and acquaintances who are practising teachers and who can be persuaded to test new material in their schools for nothing (a process now grandly known as validation).

The complex and time-eating processes through which text-

---

* London, West Riding and Kent Educational Committees buy direct through their own supply officer. Educational contractors, unlike booksellers, do not stock books and accordingly receive a modest discount from publishers – between $16\frac{1}{2}$ and 20 per cent.

books pass before arriving in the classroom locker ensure that schools cannot be hustled or hard-sold into buying sets of textbooks which they have not thoroughly examined and sampled. Orders are achieved mainly through mail-shots, since it is clearly impossible for even the most expansive publisher to cover all the thirty thousand-odd outlets. Inspection copies are solicited by schools and sent off by the publisher, and if the sample proves satisfactory a set is eventually ordered. Alternatively, and in parallel, representatives of textbook publishers, themselves often ex-school teachers or in-laws of teachers, call on schools and show their wares to a staff room that might be eager or apathetic. A small percentage of this vast profession reads educational book reviews, attends courses in the holidays and visits regional exhibitions. But most school teachers, like other human beings, settle for the easy life, and can only be induced to use a new textbook if it is actually presented to them and they don't have to bother to ask for it or send it back. Hence the practice of broadcasting the arrival of a new textbook by the distribution, free, of up to a thousand copies.

The idea for a textbook could come from a manuscript sent in by a teacher, possibly prompted by a publishers representative; or from an editor's recognition of an unsatisfied need in the educational world; or, of course, from an amalgam of both. It may be that there is a new and fashionable trend in schools towards, say, geographical fieldwork or archaeology or archives, and that existing books on the subject are negligible or dreary. It may be that the teaching of English through textbooks has become monotonous and formal and needs the stimulus of a new course. In any case a book will be talked about within the publisher's office, commissioned, or an existing manuscript re-jigged; then a version, possibly in Roneo form, will be sent round for their comments to teachers friendly to the house. Simultaneously the book will be costed by the firm's production manager, who will have to be given an idea of the print number and the price ceiling by the sales department. He must cost the book as low as possible, as the textbook field is much more sensitive than general publishing to price limits. School teachers are cautious with public money and quick to spot an overpriced book.

The economics of textbook production are completely different to the economics of general publishing, as the comparison of *The Guru and the Golf Club* and *The Alabaster Egg* and *History Alive* (see Chapter 6) illustrates. Unlike a general publisher, the textbook publisher can gain no clue to the proper print number of a new title from trade reaction to the advance distribution of jackets; he cannot expect any bunce money from the sale of rights that might accrue to a general title as described in Chapter 6. Nor can there be much of an advance sale; he may publish a book with advance orders of only 130-odd copies. He has to rely on the sensitivity of his representatives in the field and his own judgment, and be guided by the economics of book production.

Customarily the first print of a new textbook, which may be ten or twenty thousand copies, is produced at little or no profit, the profit in textbooks being in the reprints – and in the reprints and in the reprints. It may take him four or five years to sell out of his first print or, in the case of a 'hit', four or five months; he does not know which it will be. The book will only sell if it is needed, if it is well produced and if it is sensibly priced. In this way the textbook business in England is perhaps the fairest in the world; each set of books ordered for schools will have been thoroughly sampled and digested by the teacher ordering it and there is no question, as there is still in fourteen of the states in America, of lobbying or corruption on any scale whatsoever. Corruption is difficult when you have fifty thousand customers.

The rewards to authors of successful textbooks can be immense. They will rank with and surpass the earned incomes of directors of the fattest and most fee-easy public companies, and will certainly surpass those of the directors of the publishing companies for whom they 'work'. The real consistent best-sellers are not the works of Messrs Amis, Robbins, Stone and Capote, or Mesdames West, Murdoch, Spark and Brophy, but those of Flavell and Wakelam (Methuen) and Dr W. Gordon Sears (nursing books from Edward Arnold) who can earn up to ten thousand pounds a year for years and years for the same books, and the Sisters Polkingthorne Activity Geography readers (Evans). 'Janet and John', an early reading scheme current in the United States* and in Britain has sold in millions. An English course published specifically for the Nigerian market by Oxford University Press has sold three million copies so far.

This leads us to the question of the sale of textbooks overseas. A publisher and Prime Minister, Harold Macmillan, reminded us how brief an authority the British had as a global power. Within one hundred and fifty years the British bought, stole, conquered or, as in the case of Cyprus, were given, a quarter of the globe. Although since the war the red on the map has been repainted in other colours, the habit and, in many cases, the enjoyment of the English language has withstood the change. The one inalienable asset of British publishers is that they speak English. Textbooks produced in England are adapted or exported intact to every corner of the globe from Vancouver to Sydney. The more sophisticated countries of course produce their own with local publishers, and the more unsophisticated emergent African states are attempting, with the co-operation of Mr Macmillan's own firm, to do so themselves, with rather less success. The English expertise, their relative freedom from cultural chauvinism (cf. the Institut Français) and their often unsung ruthlessness abroad have led to an historic situation where children in Karachi and Cape Town have been brought up on textbooks produced in Bloomsbury.

An American invasion – their publishers are more ready to combine and to take risks, and their government and cultural foundations more ready to support them – has diminished British interest in this traditional market, especially at the university level. However, British textbooks, which have always been cheaper and could easily be brighter than their American equivalents, still have a market in these areas, where educational systems range from the refined to the haphazard. (In many African states it depends on

---

* 'Translated' by Mrs Nisbet from 'Alice and Jerry' – much used and currently much abused.

whether the Norodny Bank has sent a recent cheque.) Not even in the most refined of these countries has the textbook system reached such a level of value for money and freedom of choice, in harmony with public and private interest, as in Britain.

There are two clouds on the horizon.

British textbook publishers watched with apprehension the arrival on their scene of the Nuffield Foundation. This giant charity was infected very properly by a desire to study the needs of children and school teachers, and produced after much labour some handsome and fairly expensive science books whose sale and distribution were sub-contracted to commercial publishers (Messrs Penguins and Longmans). The Foundation has been over-taken by the National Schools Council, which has as its objective research through project work into most fields of teaching activity with a view to publishing appropriate textbooks. These, publishers are assured, will also be put out to offer to existing commercial firms. But how long will it be, some ask, with all the prestige of a national body behind them, and all the support of school teachers and local authorities, before they take to publishing themselves?

As a matter of fact the Publishers' Association wisely decided to co-operate with the Nuffield Foundation, the Schools Council and the Scottish Council in distributing the books and research that these organizations finally, after many committee meetings, produced. If they had been obdurate it is quite likely that the foundations would have bypassed the traditional textbook firms and done their own distribution. It is interesting that, in mid-1970, out of the eighteen publishers who co-operated in such schemes, probably only five have made any money out of them. Indeed, one of the privileged five publishers described the scheme that his house distributed to the School Council, as 'hazy and semi-lunatic'.

Publishers seriously regard themselves as the best purveyors of textbook material and feel that, although their chosen writers may be lower-keyed and less exotic, and that there are fewer of them per project, the results are more practical. It has been noted that after the first excitement of many of these foundation courses, the teachers tend to revert to the practical textbook which has been shown to work in classrooms.

The point might also be gently made to any Minister of Education that textbook publishers not only cost the tax-payer nothing, but actually pay taxes. On the other hand, foundations can spend up to a quarter of a million pounds on a project with no measurable saving to the community. All recognize, however, that the activity of these well-meaning people wiped a lot of sleepy-dust out of the eyes of some of the older textbook publishers and stimulated new thoughts about how children should be educated.

The second major problem facing educational publishers is the impact on schools of a variety (too great a variety) of visual aids. These range from little pieces of felt placed on a board by a teacher to make a (rough) likeness of a French village, to banks of tape recorders congregated in a language laboratory, automatic programmed teaching machines, closed-circuit TV or straightforward film projectors, not to mention at least five competing variations of TV cassettes. Any device which takes the teaching strain away from the teacher and enables the children to proceed by themselves at their own speed with a delectable piece of equipment should be welcome, but there are two snags. The teacher is constitutionally, one could almost say emotionally, attached to the idea that teaching is a matter of personal communication between him or herself and the children. Any reference at the annual dinner of the National Union of Teachers to 'the sacrament of teaching' will be greeted with a roar of approval, and denigratory remarks about teaching machines are drowned in applause.

Then there is the cost. Few of these machines are standardized,★ and local authorities have often been caught by salesmen who have landed them with a lot of hardware and accoutrements which gather dust in their store cupboards, and cannot be paid for except by special allowances. The capitation for books in British

★ At the time of going to press there were forty-five contestants in the (battle)field of video cassettes. Only a few will survive.

G

schools is too little to cover the cost even of necessary books, and no amount of ingenious machinery can replace the communion of the reader with the printed word. The rich and spoilt countries of the West may be seduced by the lure of machinery to supplement or replace their class books with more expensive props, but anyone who has seen Kenyans gazing into the windows of book shops with something like hunger in their eyes, or seen a silent classroom in a Bantu school poring over expensively acquired textbooks of their very own, cannot doubt that publishers have not only a long run ahead of them but also, in this last case, a duty to perform.

# 9

## Publishing in the United States

Americans are numerous, breezy and rich, and one would expect the American publishing scene to be different from the English. It is different, both in tempo and scale, but not, as we shall see, *that* different.

Mr Bob Gottlieb, a luminary or whizz-kid with Simon & Schuster, decamps to join Alfred Knopf. Simon & Schuster is (or was) the bazaziest imprint in New York, with a higher average of best-sellers than most, but it nevertheless consistently makes a tiny loss on general books (see Chapter 6). Gottlieb takes with him to Knopf (which is owned by Random House, which in turn is owned by R.C.A., one of the biggest corporations in the world), his 'wardrobe of writers'.* Possibly he moves for more money, or for stock options and, fringe benefits or, just as likely, he is bored with S. & S. On arriving he is asked by the personnel lady what kind of typewriter he would like his secretary to use. 'Oh,' says Gottlieb modestly, 'any old typewriter.' '*Old* typewriter,' she mutters. Finally they manage to locate an old typewriter, and the editor's whim, as it appears, is gratified.

The American publishing industry has grown so big that most individual imprints have been practically submerged and are now barely recognizable as individual members of a conglomerate. As firms have merged and been taken over, so the personality of the editor/publisher grows in importance, for idiosyncratic and possibly dilatory as he may be, the editor has become the pivotal

* About twenty, including Joseph Heller (*Catch-22*), Doris Lessing and Jessica Mitford.

figure in the business, because he alone can produce the product –
the book. The vortex of superstar editors moving from house to
house spins off a trail of broken loyalties and higher advances.
This movement has become so dizzy that one day the editors may
stabilize and offer *their* authors to the revolving publishers.

Wall Street, it is said, looked at publishing and it was love at
first sight. Here was a growth industry which was socially O.K.
and, until recently, made relatively recession-proof by Federal
spending. And what spending. In 1968 Holt, Rinehart and Winston sold over four hundred thousand copies of three music books
to the state of California. Not only the money men but also
corporations in other media moved in. Since the Sherman Act,
which, along with the Federal Control Commission exists to see
that big corporations do not dominate any one field, diversifica-
tion in America is often politically impelled. It can also be done
for kicks, as when a car-park company buys a literary agency.

So C.B.S. owns Holt, Rinehart and Winston; Time-Life owns
Little, Brown; Xerox owns the Ginn Text Book Company;
Litton Industries own Van Nostrand; the National General Corporation has bought Grosset & Dunlap, an institutional children's
book outfit, and the Times Mirror chain owns the New American
Library and World. Of course federal spending is politically controlled and changes with the administration: Democrats are
traditionally lavish, Republicans severe. Many big school and
textbook companies have shown losses under the Republican
Administration, and sharp withdrawal of funds for new educational schemes from New York publishers has led Wall Street not
to fall out of love with publishers but to recognize that the honey-
moon is over. The allocation, often of millions of dollars, for
school programmes offered by the Democrats has simply frozen,
cooling the feet of the corporations who have moved in to
publishing.

The headquarters of a giant publishing corporation is a limbless
brain – management, editorial and publicity – occupying a floor
or two of a midtown or downtown Manhatten skyscraper. A few
of the older publishers like Harper and Row, Scribner's and

Macmillan's have their own buildings, but mostly New York publishing is lateral, air-conditioned and, with the strong exception of Scribner's, Jewish. All the mechanical work of inventory, selling and accountancy will be done in a suburb, or perhaps even in Chicago.

The money which has poured into American publishing from Wall Street and from the acquisitive corporations in the last decade is in pursuit of growth, and growth they must have, annually. So too many books are published, no question about it, and most disappear without a sigh, losing money for all involved. Pressure comes from without: the budget for trade sales must be larger each year, more titles, more gross dollars, more net income, more, more each year; success makes it tougher since that has to be topped next time around. And the stock price must be up, an impression of expansion and growth must be maintained regardless, or Wall Street will lose interest; this is of the utmost importance and must never be forgotten when thinking of any of the publicly owned houses, which is practically everybody. Raymond C. Hagel,* president of Crowell-Collier Macmillan, is essentially a business operator rather than a publisher; his regular acquisition of other companies succeeded in reviving what appeared to be a quiescent corporation and raising the price of its stock. And pressure comes from within: an editor's salary, title, status, prestige, future authors, all depend on the books he does and their success. Consequently he is inclined to over-produce, sign up everything and anything, take chances, hope that one or two will click, play with company money since they'll allow for failures as long as he turns out a money-maker regularly. If he succeeds he can expect to move on and up for more money to another house. If he fails ... In either case he will be hired or fired by a forty-ish admin. or finance company man, without publishing chromosomes. Hence the remark of one of the few independents – Mike Bessie of Atheneum: 'What's so strange about corporations behaving like corporations?'

Everything about American publishing is bigger except,

* 'We are not a conglomerate; we are a cultural congeneracy.'

significantly, the number of titles published annually. The print numbers are bigger, the discounts, the salaries and the retail prices are all bigger. The annual volume of Cromwell-Collier Macmillan (admittedly including all sorts of ancillaries in the media like the Berlitz School) exceeds the total volume of all British publishers, and when the president, Raymond Hagel, and his right-hand man, Jerry Kaplan, go 'shopping' in London, independent British publishers tremble with excitement. On their 1968–9 trips they bought Studio Vista from Lord (Tim) Beaumont, Cleaverhume Press from Macmillan & Co., Geoffrey Chapman, an Australian with a neat line in Catholic school books, and Cassells, the latter for two million pounds.

A book published in Britain at £1·95 becomes in the States a far handsomer object, printed on better paper and with a thicker binding, at $6.95; and it stands a chance, if it gets into the best-seller brigade, of selling up to ten times as many copies. So *Myra Breckinridge* by Gore Vidal might sell fifteen thousand in Britain and the Commonwealth and one hundred and fifty thousand in the United States of America; originally British titles like *The Naked Ape* or Antonia Fraser's *Mary Queen of Scots* will many times outdo the British sales figures when they hit the U.S. best-seller lists. And then there is the relative lack of censorship, which prompted the sale of so many Grove Press titles like *My Secret Life*, *The Pearl* and *Norman Douglas' Limericks*. The difference in the paperback world is even more spectacular; the first print of Elia Kazan's *The Arrangement*, published by a new arrival on the New York scene, Sol Stein of Stein & Day, sold in paperback two and a half million copies. In the U.K. the equivalent would be between fifty and a hundred thousand.

American book buyers are not dissimilar to the British – middle-class, white, aged between thirty-five and sixty – only there are more of them. Year after year, since the war, the best-seller lists have been made up of commercial fiction like *Valley of the Dolls*, non-controversial non-fiction like *The Secret of Santa Vittoria*, cosy ideology often of a self-congratulatory religious kind, cook books, books of self-help – *How to Make a Million*

*Dollars on the Stock Exchange* – and soft-bellied non-fiction like *The Joys of Yiddish*. This market is reached through traditional methods – bookstalls, book clubs* and cut-price outlets. (N.B. The American market is not restricted by the net book agreement which applies in England and prevents publishers from giving savagely handsome discounts through book clubs and simultaneous publication, or through selling books in cut-price wholesale outlets.) Apart from this long-standing public which is prepared to pay $6.95 for a novel, or $10.00 for a non-fiction book, there is a profitable spin-off from increased Federal spending on education in the kind of cross-pollinated 'think' books of which Jason Epstein's Anchor Books (Doubleday) are the first and finest example. This 'campus market' as it is often called is annually refuelled by bored young middle-class housewives.

Buying is stimulated by the desire to conform, and to get on the best-seller list is much more of a shit or bust affair than in England. The best-seller lists published by the *Publishers' Weekly* are reasonably accurate and list the number of copies in print and the number of weeks on the best-seller list. There being no national newspapers in the United States, the book pages of the big city journals like the *New York Times* and the *Los Angeles Times* are crucial. In New York it's important for publishers to be in with the reviewing establishment which is often referred to as the Jewish Mafia, and TV exposure is even more significant than in England. But often a book will defy the normal processes and mysteriously start to sell, and is then referred to by the mystified square publishers as an 'underground' best-seller. Its subject may well be macrobiotics, Jewish mysticism, draft dodging or zany humour; at any rate its theme will appeal to the under-thirty-fives. This is often called the 'underground market', not to be confused with the campus market.

There is in America a huge untapped market which could absorb a controversial paperback at, say $1.95, but which has not

---

* The U.S.A. is big enough and rich enough for minority tastes to be big business. Apart from the middle-brow giants like the Book of the Month Club and the Literary Guild, selection for which makes author and publisher a fortune, there are book clubs for professional men and women, sportsmen and even homosexuals.

yet been scientifically researched. There is a fortune to be made here. In the meantime most big houses maintain a bright young man with a licence to turn out freaky and radical titles like *The Diary of a Nigger-Loving Commie-Jew Beatnik*, which, of course, must be profitable. In England publishers have so far not catered for the kind of public which is loyal to and purchases regularly journals like the *International Times*, *Oz* and *Private Eye* (all, needless to say, undistributed by Messrs W. H. Smith). The time will come.

To the pained European lefty, American domestic and foreign policies sometimes appear to be controlled by the prejudices of oil millionaires, armament manufacturers, dyspeptic New York taxi drivers and nigger-hating demagogues. But America is still a free enough country for these qualities to be criticized, and there is no freer medium than that of book publishing. Let us then end on a hopeful note and quote the reasons a young editor gave for being in the business. He is Alan Rinzler, formerly of Holt, Rinehart & Winston, now the publisher of Rolling Stone Books, in California.

> ... there is an increasing body of people who are vocally telling the truth about American society. My job is to make myself available to them, find them, help them get it together and then through the giant resources of my (oh, how this disturbs me more every day) capitalistic corporation, promulgate it throughout the country: students, laymen, young people, the intellectuals and ruling class (hopefully) THEN pray it makes some difference in the way things are.

# 10

## Issues of the Day: Defamation and Obscenity

Publishing in Britain is ill-equipped to face the problems of the 'seventies for reasons which I hope have become clear in earlier chapters. Briefly the difficulties are (1) The relatively small size of the trade (£150 million) and the net decline of public and private spending on books in the home market. (2) The multiplicity of titles, which shows no sign of abating. (3) The economic plight of the booksellers, who, undermanned and under-capitalized, unable to pay high-street rents, find it difficult to work on their margin. When a highly efficient little shop like the Nancy Leigh Bookshop in Woking can only scrape a living on a turnover of thirty thousand pounds a year, and, at the other end, Dillon's University Bookshop, equally well run, fails to make a profit on a turnover of a million, things must be bad.

Manufacturers of any kind face similar economic difficulties, but since they are not marketing opinions, comment or information none face the controversial and – because it so often impinges upon freedom – important issue of defamation.

### Defamation

In company with other purveyors of the printed word, publishers must constantly be alert to the risk of libel. Although author, publisher, printer and sometimes bookseller are all responsible at law for putting out a libel, it is usually the publisher and author who are sued, and the publisher who ends up paying the damages. Despite the standard clause in every publishing contract whereby an author warrants that there is nothing libellous in his manuscript, and undertakes to indemnify the publisher in the case of legal action, publishers seldom collect from authors. This is partly because they wish to remain on good terms, partly because the author rarely has enough money to pay, and sometimes because the indemnity clause is not legally enforceable in the particular case.

The damages allowed by the courts are rarely as great as those inflicted upon newspapers, or as punitive as the five-thousand-pound award plus about four thousand costs against *Private Eye* in the Russell of Liverpool case. Nevertheless, it is a mistake to imagine that publishers relish a libel action because it brings publicity, and therefore sales, to their books. On the contrary, a forthcoming libel action may oblige them to withdraw the offending book from sale, and if they lose the action they have to undertake the costly business of correcting the copies. Besides few publishers have the neurotic energy or desire to spend time in the courts of justice, and however good the publisher's case, the costs of defence are so high that it is probably cheaper for him to settle for a token amount and an apology.

Unlike newspapers, who find it cheaper to maintain their own libel lawyer on the premises, a publisher may insure against the possibility of a defamatory libel suit, and this will cost the Second Eleven publisher, always assuming he has never made a substantial claim, about five hundred pounds a year in premiums. It is, of course, impossible to insure against obscene libel, which is a criminal offence.

Since the Harold Lever amendments to the libel laws (1959) the publisher must be most sensitive in the area of non-fiction. If, for example, in a novel about a repertory company there is a red-headed actress who appears to be somewhat free with her favours, it is most unlikely that she has a red-headed namesake in a real repertory company, and even if she does she will no longer have cause to bring action against the novelist or publisher. There is a far greater risk of libel in a book on, say, the current political scene. Take the case of *The British Political Fringe* (George Thayer). In spite of its excellent jacket, which won the publisher an international award, the book did not sell at all well – but it did attract twenty-three libel actions.

We know what small fry publishers are in commercial terms, and if they are attacked for defamation, and the suit is expensively and savagely pursued, they could be broken on one case. Heavy damages can rock a newspaper, but an uninsured publisher could be sunk: the forty thousand pounds paid by the Mirror Group to Lord Boothby resulted in an assistant editor being sacked, but the next morning the paper came out; the sum would wreck all but the top twenty London publishers.*

However, a crusade can make a book. Publishers like a thundering exposé; it makes them feel like little guardians of the public's right to defend itself, and the book usually sells. In the 'thirties Gollancz made his name with political polemics: now the climate in quieter and a publisher must look for more practical targets for his crusades. Significantly, it was one of New York's smaller publishers, Dick Grossman, who published a crucial book in Ralph Nader's *Unsafe at any Speed*, a survey of safety in motor cars. After publication Ralph Nader was hounded, trailed and persecuted by General Motors right up to Congress, where his hearing was a triumph. Finding no evidence of a dissolute heterosexual life, his opponents asked at one point why he had dedicated his book to a man. 'Because', replied Nader, 'he became a paraplegic as a result of an automobile accident.' As a direct result of the enormous publicity and readership this book gained, Congress introduced new laws requiring alterations in automobile design. Nader had proved conclusively, inch by inch, bolt by bolt and screw by screw, how carelessly and callously motor manufacturers had neglected the safety factor in their product, and

* A record forty thousand pounds damages was awarded to Captain Broome, R.N., against the publisher Cassell and their author David Irving, and was upheld in the Court of Appeal.

demonstrated how very little of their time, money and research was spent on making motor cars safe. He became a national hero.* America's most powerful lobby, the automobile industry, was defeated by one man with one book, and this required courage from the publisher.

While British interests are not quite so ruthless in their own defence, a publisher presented with a manuscript as passionate and as detailed as Nader's on, say, safety in the aircraft industry, would have to proceed carefully to avoid legal action. The book might claim, for example, that an air crash due to the pilot's misjudgment of his height was in turn due to the company's failure to instal a two-way radio altimeter. Unless it was substantiated, this charge would be highly libellous; the merits of such an instrument would have to be endorsed by independent aeronautical engineers, its efficacy supported by pilots, and so forth. If the book contained other allegations of aircraft manufacturers' and airlines, indifference to passengers' safety, and their preference, in allocating revenue, for advertising over safety measures, then a whole battery of independent experts would have to be corralled to provide the book with its necessary protection in the courts of law. So a publisher embarking on even a heavily documented attack on a powerful interest should provide himself (for they will probably go for him and not the author) with indisputable technical evidence.

As for libel of the defamatory kind, no sane publisher would court prosecution: the case nearly always comes too late to help the sale of the book, the expense is enormous, and the pleasure of being able to lecture a jury from the box on the virtues of freedom, momentary.

---

* Unfortunately, owing to a (typical) publishing quirk, the book was not taken by a British publisher. This was because the Grossman edition had sold substantially to Australia, and most British publishers felt bound by the Publishers' Association Agreement which prescribes that a publisher must have all traditional British market rights; or perhaps they felt that the gilt had been taken off the gingerbread. Dick Grossman (now under Viking's umbrella) reports, incidentally, that the moment Nader won his case, his book stopped selling.

## Obscenity

The twentieth century, having discovered sex, is disposed to linger upon it. The mass media are sodden with sex: the angle at which a proud wife proffers a fountain pen to her husband in an advertisement is intentionally erotic in some remote way, and even candy for kids has a suggestive shape, or so we are told by the psychiatrists.

Writers relish sexual descriptions as much as their readers do, and while the current relative freedom of expression has induced a degree of satiety, and it is no longer simply a matter of the higher the sex content the higher the sales, there is no doubt that sex helps to sell books. Attitudes have changed in and out of courts of law. A few years ago, *By Love Possessed*, that exquisitely complicated and often obscure novel by James Gould Cozzens, was about to be published by Longmans when it was discovered that on page 189 THE WORD had been spelt out in full. This caused a furore, and W. H. Smith were in doubt as to whether this obviously literary novel could be distributed. On the strength of this excitement a great number of copies were sold, although not necessarily read.

Some kinds of sex sell better than others. Sadism has always been a staple British hobby, and books are often bought for the wrong reasons. One publisher had just put out an English translation of *Un Camp Très Ordinaire* under the title *Ravensbruck*, the touching and appalling story of a women's concentration camp. He saw it in the hands of a taxi-driver waiting for a fare in Piccadilly, and, delighted by this evidence that his wares were reaching the public, he approached the reader and asked his opinion. 'Oh, it's all right, but why aren't there any pictures?'

If sadism is acceptable, necrophilia is not, as Aleister Crowley discovered. More recently a book was turned down by a publisher even after it had been set up in print, because the conclusion was necrophilic in tenor. The author refused to change this episode into a more routine and acceptable sex murder, and the book went to another publisher. The latter described the incident to a

Cambridge undergraduate and he in turn reported the details in full in *Granta*. The indiscreet publisher was told that he had libelled the discreet publisher, and had to apologize. (The undergraduate was David Frost.)

Other than by sounding out Counsel, there is no way in which a publisher can get any reasonable assurance that he will not be prosecuted for obscenity in a given book. Legal advisers tend to advise against publication. A few months before the publication of the Casement Diaries a Queen's Counsel declared that it was not only obscene but could not be published because it was the property of the Crown.* *The Casement Diaries* could not, continued this eminent Council, even be published in France, for there was an agreement over such matters between the British and French governments.

It was published in France and then sold to America, but only when a Member of Parliament actually waved a copy of it at the Home Secretary in the House of Commons was it published in London. The Diaries – still considered a forgery by Irish patriots – are a rather dreary recital of the sufferings of a galloping sodomite, interspersed with touches of self-pity and occasional heroic modesty. Published by Sidgwick & Jackson in 1959 as *The Black Diaries*, the book was never prosecuted.

The most successful case in recent times, and one which changed the pattern of publishing, was of course that of *Lady Chatterley's Lover*. Not so much a court case, more of a rout. No one appeared to be on the Crown's side; even the *Spectator* refused permission for Prosecuting Counsel to search their files for opinions of the 'thirties. It was a splendidly organized affair, with bishops and professors denouncing the Crown for not recognizing true morality. *Lady Chatterley* sold a couple of million copies and Sir Allen Lane floated triumphantly on the stock exchange.

Few publishers have such resources, or such a good case, as had

* Singleton-Gates, a crime reporter on the *Evening News*, was given a copy of the Diaries by a commissioner of police over lunch at the Café Royal in the 'twenties. It became Singleton-Gates's crusade to see the book recognized as an authentic document, and published. Until publication, successive Home Secretaries either denied the existence of the manuscript or implied that it was a forgery.

Sir Allen with *Lady Chatterley*, and should a novel be deemed obscene in a magistrates court the publisher would be more prudent financially to leave it at that, shrug his shoulders and wait for the inevitable change of climate. Before the decade is out we shall probably see published in England some books which have been successful in other parts of the world, and which probably have literary merit too, such as *l'Histoire de l'Oeil*,* though their publication now would very likely provoke an obscenity case.

The case of literary freedom in England and Wales was wittily and cogently argued by Benn Levy, the playwright and former M.P. for Slough, who in July 1969 wrote the report of the Arts Council Committee on this question. The previous year a semi-public meeting had been held to which parties known to be interested had been invited (unfortunately Mary Whitehouse was *not*). A committee had been appointed to examine the question and present a recommendation which would be handed on to the then Home Secretary, Mr James Callaghan. As the month wound on and the 'expert' evidence rolled in, it became clear to the members of the committee, by no means a bawdy bunch of men, that the existing laws were unworkable, nay, ridiculous, and that since it was difficult to draw the line between what was obscene and what was not it might be more appropriate to abolish the line altogether. The Danish experience was noted: when restraints on pornography had been totally relaxed, sales quivered to a high spot, then sunk as a result of public apathy. Also worth noting was the fact that the sex-crime rate during this period dropped by 25 per cent in Copenhagen. Of course this is an area in which people are inclined to disregard statistics. Everyone who speaks on the subject appears to have a fifteen-year-old daughter who could or could not be – both sides are emphatic – affected by pornography. A handsome young grandmother, Mary Whitehouse, who may or may not be supported by less unsophisticated parties like Moral Re-armament, is a formidable and emotional advocate of imposed decency. No amount of reasoning such as that contained

* No, not the *Histoire d'O*, by Pauline Réage, which was published quietly in 1970 in England by Maurice Girodias's Olympia Press as *The Story of O*.

in the Arts Council Working Report – which calls for total abolition of censorship – can shake her conviction. And anyway, it is doubtful whether any sane and clear-cut proposal like the abolition of all legal restraint would pass through both Houses of Parliament.

Very few publishers are pornographers (sales of the hard-core stuff are really quite modest, incidentally), but most, save Sir Basil Blackwell, who in his seventy-ninth year said in evidence that by reading *Last Exit to Brooklyn* he had been scarred for life, would probably feel disposed towards the abolitionist case. It is sad and not untypical of the public that of all aspects of publishing, pornography excites the greatest interest.

More troubling than in the home market is the censorship which still obtains in Australia and South Africa, countries which between them take a good whack of British publishers' export business. In Australia censorship is handled on a national basis and the publisher has to rely on the good sense of his agent in deciding how hard to press should the Commonwealth Censorship Board refuse a book entry. In South Africa censorship is widespread, unchallengable and, at the lowest level, where illiterate and redundant Customs men rummage through booksellers' parcels, grotesque. Yes, they really did once ban *Black Beauty*, and the list of books unavailable to South Africans is almost as long as the British National Bibliography. A publisher must recognize that almost any modern novel with a fair quota of what used to be called outspoken language or scenes, irrespective of any treatment of the colour question, will automatically and irrevocably be banned in that Republic.

When British law on obscenity was changed to admit literary merit as grounds for defence, an unofficial channel to the attorney general's office was opened. A publisher could present to that office his intentions on a book he wished to print, together with the names of those who had undertaken to give evidence in its defence should it be prosecuted. Equally unofficially would come the reply that provided the publisher did not exploit the work too blatantly, probably no action would be taken against him. Thus

*Lolita* was published, and Henry Miller's *Tropic of Cancer* – which, incidentally, was so successful that it wiped out all the earlier losses its publisher John Calder had incurred in his pursuit of literature – and also Jean Genet's first prose work *Our Lady of the Flowers*, of which a printer once remarked to the publisher, 'Shall I burn it or will you?' Publishers must bear in mind, also, that a 20p or 30p edition may be banned or prosecuted whereas its hardback parent has gone scot free. Paperback publishers have complained that there's one law for the rich and another for the poor, but of course the law is taking into account the fact that a cheap edition will be much more widely disseminated than an expensive hardbound edition.

A publisher with a penchant for bold or impertinent books may be subject to private pressures which can amount to censorship of a different kind. A partner or co-director who is supposed to be sleeping might suddenly wake up to the fact that he is associated with a publication which could be offensive to the government, the royal family, the Church of England, the state of Israel or any other institution he is anxious to keep in with.

Again, censorship often masquerades as 'good taste'. Some years ago *Figaro* serialized the adventures of a Stern Gang assassin, who admitted that he had joined that poetic (Abraham Stern was a poet) and bloodthirsty organization because (a) he was a good shot, and (b) he needed the money. On its publication in book form in England, the British press was silent, save Richard Crossman who congratulated the publisher on his boldness. A Sunday newspaper had agreed to serialize it, but the board of directors had overruled the editor on the grounds that it would offend their Jewish public. It was embarrassing, and perhaps the book should not have been published. But who's to say? Publishing should be a fiery and not a soothing business.

Quite often a book will be quietly censored by W. H. Smith & Sons. W. H. Smith are not only the biggest, and indeed seemingly ubiquitous, retailers of books in England, they are also the largest wholesalers of paperbacks and daily newspapers (which, some snide people think, prohibits their getting a damaging press).

H

By their own accounting they reckon to sell at leaast a sixth of the printed number of a big book. If the buyers at Smith's fancy a title they can make it into a best-seller, and enthusiasm from this organization can push a projected publication into a reprint at proof stage. Paul Hamlyn for one could not have made his million(s) without the support of Smith's. But a refusal by this near-monopoly organization to handle a book with strong sales possibilities could mean a big revenue loss for the publisher, who, unlike *Private Eye* for example, has few alternative outlets. The smaller publisher with a difficult or perhaps mildly obscene title is appalled by Smith's businesslike – and to that extent understandable – preoccupation with best-sellers and steadies of the kind we see on sale at provincial branches. Vainly do the furious young Davids rain their smooth hard pebbles at the bland Goliath; he smiles and goes trundling on.*

The power of W. H. Smith to stifle even the most significant publication by simply declining to stock it is so unchallenged that it might be in the public interest to investigate their methods and reasoning. It is sometimes argued, for example by those in the Defence of Literature and the Arts Society, that a distributive organization of such size has a duty to the public beyond that of the normal merchant, and that if they cannot order doubtful and difficult books, at least they should supply single copies to customers on request. It is an unpleasant fact that in August 1970, out of the numerous novels that were published, W. H. Smith decided to 'support' (i.e. stock and subscribe) only thirty-two. Moreover, Smith's appear to arrive at their decision to 'ban' a book from their shops rather uncertainly, and have been known to change their minds with titles that subsequently became best-sellers.

In defence of Smith's, it must be said that no commercial enterprise can be dictated to as to what it should stock, and one can hardly blame them if they find that to rationalize their business they must sell more of the goods people want, like

* For details of Goliath's blandness see C. H. Rolph, *Books in the Dock* (André Deutsch, London, 1969), pp. 123-4.

gramophone records and typewriters, and less of those they don't. None the less, Smith's say that their book sales have increased as much as their profits, which have been not unspectacular. Besides, they might well add, as a large organization they have a duty to protect the public from subversion or corruption, and, like the publisher, they are vulnerable to prosecution by offended parties on grounds of defamation or obscenity.

To end on a more hopeful note, it is interesting that during the same period, 1969–70, Messrs C. and A. (the organization roughly equivalent to Smith's in South Africa) lowered their overheads, increased their profits, and also increased their turnover of books, which leads one to suggest that there may be growing markets for British books overseas. More aggressive selling abroad is definitely one of the prescriptions for British publishers if they are to survive the 'seventies.

This decade will certainly see more mergers, more takeovers, and more straightforward failures, but there will also be rationalization and co-operation among publishers over publicity and over the simplification of their odd little trade. And there will still be nothing to stop anybody with a bit of money, a lot of enthusiasm, energy and powers of persuasion from putting up his plate and becoming a publisher.

*London* 1971

# APPENDIX I

## The Real Best-Sellers

In September 1968 Alex Hamilton ('Pooter' of *The Times*, a top sleuth of the publishing business) published a list and analysis of the real best-sellers, most of which is reproduced here with his and their permission.

Though his intention was partly to demolish the accuracy of the best-seller lists which appear in the press, it is effective as a statistical sketch of the pattern of publishing both here and America which is likely to continue for some years. He does not claim to show the turnover of each title, nor the profitability nor, of course, can there be an analysis of the rights revenue. The discerning scanner will note that though sales of Alan Williams's novel published by Blond were modest, this would have more potential in other countries than the University of London Press's English course for Libya which, presumably, could only be sold in Libya to Libyans. NB. Government contracts, whether for books or missiles, are always good business. Quoth Pooter:

> Take the Bible and a hymnbook, three dictionaries, a grammar, a cookbook, a logbook, a sex book and a non-book and you have a best-seller list – this week, next week, any week. From a compiler's viewpoint this makes a damn dull serial, so he leaves these out.
>
> He also leaves out many others, as my table of the 1968 lead sellers of over 50 major publishers shows.
>
> He is bound to. He is fishing for marlin with a bent pin,

and catching trout. Even in fiction back-list selling is the basis of publishing turnover. Every year, for instance, these huge accumulated sales accumulate more: *Gone with the Wind*, 936,961; *Tess of the d'Urbervilles*, 598,651; *Kim*, 592,832; and for children Enid Blyton's *River of Adventure*, 136,661 (Macmillan); *Under Milk Wood* has reached 160,000 (Dent); the Orwell leader is *1984*, 75,000, and soon Secker and Warburg will add four volumes of essays and letters to a continuously selling Orwell *œuvre*. Bodley Head add an annual 5,000 to 7,000 of the world's best seller, Dr Spock.

Nor are they all classics: 8,500 this year for *H.M.S. Ulysses* brings the figure up to 356,000; 6000 for *Doctor Zhivago* makes the score 462,000 (Collins).

Current best-seller lists are sales aids and therefore vulnerable to jobbery. Also to muddle: publishers, who know the truth, are held not to be very free with it, while booksellers, who often do not know it, are likely to urge titles they have over-ordered, like waiters pushing 'the chef's special dish'. Where their motives are pure, it is not clear if they are based on stock sales, or inspiration.

Of 41,000 bookselling outlets about 5,000 are regularly concerned with hard-cover books, so to take a dozen samples is neither enough nor nationally representative. This helps to explain why, for instance, of Hutchinson's six top sellers this this year, all over 15,000, only number three (Wheatley's new novel) has shown in any chart.

| Publisher | Title | Author | 1968 Sale | Listed | Notes |
|---|---|---|---|---|---|
| Adlard Coles | Instant Weather Forecasting | Alan Watts | 14,551 | Yes | Listed only by Financial Times. |
| Allen & Unwin | Autobiography Vol. 2 | Bertrand Russell | 24,213 | Yes | Published in April. |
| W. H. Allen | In God's Underground | Richard Wurmbrand | 10,000 | No | Story of Lutheran priest in Rumania. |
| Allman | Intermediate English Grammar | Davidson and Alcock | 100,000 | No | First published 1876. Total : 2 million. |
| Bancroft | Bobtail Books | | 12,360 | No | 5p. each. 24 varieties. |
| Ernest Benn | White Witch of Rosehall | H. G. de Lissier | 5,970 | No | West Indian fiction. Annually 10,000. |
| Ernest Benn (juvenile) | Hello Lucy | Donald Bisset | 81,503 | No | |
| Anthony Blond (educ.) | English Through Experience | Albert Rowe | 3,528 | No | Through educational contractors. |
| Anthony Blond | The Brotherhood | Alan Williams | 14,000 | No | Novel. |
| Bodley Head | Ulysses | James Joyce | 5,000 | No | 'The Book of the Film.' |
| Burke's Peerage | International Yearbook | | 35,000 | No | £945 reference. |
| Burns & Oates | A New Catechism | Bishops of Netherlands | 4,200 | No | £1·75 translation. |
| Calder & Boyars | Marat/Sade | Peter Weiss | 28,278 | No | First published 1965. |
| Cambridge Univ. Press | School Mathematics Project | Bryan Thwaites (Director) | | No | First published 1965. |
| Cambridge Univ. Press | Smuts, Vol. 2, 1919-50 | W. K. Hancock | 4,167 | No | Published February. |
| Cape | Teach Your Baby to Read | Glenn Doman | 9,000* | No | Averaged 1,000 a month since 1965. |
| Cassell | Richer Than All His Tribe | Nicholas Monsarrat | 40,894† | Yes | Published August. |
| Chatto & Windus | Principles of Physics | M. Nelkon | 25,632 | No | First published 1951. |
| Chatto & Windus | Little Black Sambo | Helen Bannerman | 25,421 | No | Nostalgia? White backlash? |
| Chatto & Windus | The Nice and the Good | Iris Murdoch | 21,299 | Yes | Novel, published January. |
| Wm. Collins | The Bible (all editions) | | 1½m. | No | Ruby edition : 260,000. |
| Wm. Collins | English Dictionary | | 530,000 | No | |
| Wm. Collins | Send Down a Dove | Charles McHardy | 25,052 | Yes | Novel, published July |
| Wm. Collins | Reach for the Sky | Paul Brickhill | 19,200 | No | First published 1956. Total 422,520. |
| Wm. Collins (juvenile) | The Cat in the Hat | Dr Seuss | 18,252 | No | First published 1958. Total 156,000. |
| Constable | Tobias and the Angel | James Bridie | 10,294 | No | Set book. |
| Darton, Longman & Todd | The Jerusalem Bible | | 15,000 | No | £5. World sale since 1967 : 200,000. |
| Peter Davies | Christy | Katherine Marshall | 12,675 | No | |

| Publisher | Title | Author | | | Notes |
|---|---|---|---|---|---|
| Dawson's of Pall Mall | Statutes of the Realm | | 250 | No | £300. |
| Dent | English Pronouncing Dictionary | | 24,800 | No | First published 1918. Total ½ million. |
| Dent | Poems | Dylan Thomas | 7,000 | No | First published 1954. Total : 135,000. |
| André Deutsch | Philby | Page, Leitch, Knightley | 25,000 | Yes | +Book Club : 14,000. |
| Dobson (juvenile) | Boys and Girls of History | R. and E. Power | 4,000 | No | First published 1928. |
| Eyre & Spottiswoode | The Heritage | F. Parkinson Keyes | 17,851 | Yes | Novel. |
| Eyre & Spottiswoode | The Crying Game | John Braine | 12,265 | Yes | Published August. |
| Faber & Faber | Tunc | Lawrence Durrell | 25,973 | Yes | Published in April. |
| Faber & Faber | The Nurses' Dictionary | | 5,247 | No | |
| Folio Press | The Horrid Novels | | 1,255 | No | £17·85 set of seven. First published 1793-8. |
| Leslie Frewin | When the Sweet Talking's Done | Robin Douglas-Home | 8,555 | No | Novel. |
| Guinness | Book of Records | | 158,891 | Yes | Print order 1968 : 210,000. |
| Robert Hale | Caroline the Queen | Jean Plaidy | 11,050 | No | Historical romance. Published June. |
| Hamish Hamilton | The American Challenge | Servan Schreiber | 10,000 | Yes | Published in July. |
| Hamish Hamilton | The Day of the Feast | Margaret Lane | 20,000 | Yes | Includes Book Club. |
| Hamlyn Group | Cookery in Colour | | 22,000 | No | |
| Hamlyn (juvenile) | Bedtime Book of 365 Stories | | 15,000 | No | |
| Heinemann | Tower of Babel | Morris West | 60,106 | Yes | Present 1968 overall fiction leader. |
| Heinemann (juvenile) | Manx Mouse | Paul Gallico | 13,120 | No | |
| Heinemann (educ.) | Ordinary Level Physics | A. S. Abbott | 40,000 | No | 1967 sale : 57,700. |
| Hodder & Stoughton | The Instrument | John O'Hara | 14,000 | Yes | Novel. Published in May. |
| Hutchinson | Manchester Utd. Football Book | | 34,441 | No | Tottenham coming up well too. +60,000 Book Club. |
| Hutchinson | 20th Century Encyclopaedia | | 40,000 | No | |
| Longman's | The Gods are not Mocked | Anna Taylor | 4,011 | No | First Novel. Reprinting. |
| Longman's (educ.) | Pleasure in English | Yglesias and others | 100,000+ | No | 6-book series. ½ million since 1963. |
| Macdonald | War Planes of Second World War | William Green | 20,058 | No | |
| | Report from Iron Mountain | Anon. | 8,003 | Yes | |
| Macgibbon & Kee | Filmgoers' Companion (revised) | Leslie Halliwell | 6,726 | No | £3·15 First published 1965. |
| Macmillan (educ.) | Logarithmic and other tables | F. Castle | 150,851 | No | First published 1908. 1967 sale : 197,530. |
| Macmillan | The Public Image | Muriel Spark | 16,300 | Yes | Published in July. |

| Publisher | Title | Author | 1968 Sale | Listed | Notes |
|---|---|---|---|---|---|
| Macmillan | Survival of the Fittest | Pamela Hansford Johnson | 11,050 | Yes | Published May. |
| Methuen | The Wind in the Willows | Kenneth Graham | 13,557 | No | First published 1909. |
| Methuen | The Sociology of Education | P. W. Musgrave | 10,700 | No | All 1968 Pooh editions : 180,534. |
| Methuen | Winnie the Pooh | A. A. Milne | 10,375 | No | Total sale over 100,000. |
| Mills & Boon | Better Cookery | Aileen King | 12,000 | No | Simultaneous paperback : 32,000. |
| Muller | Bedside and Birthday Books | Patience Strong | 7,600 | No | 20th impression since 1925. |
| Oxford Univ. Press | Songs of Praise (all editions) | | 522,026 | No | +Pocket edition : 218,000. |
| Oxford Univ. Press | Concise Oxford Dictionary | | 241,025 | No | |
| Pelham Books | Pears Encyclopaedia | | 112,000 | Yes | |
| The Penguin Press | Human Aggression | Anthony Storr | 4,200 | Yes | Published in July. |
| Pitman | Economics | Frederick Benham | 8,022 | No | First published 1936. |
| Purnell | Happy Birthday Books | | 1¼m. | No | 12½p. each. |
| | Brownie Annual | | 95,000 | No | First published in 1903. 29th impression. 1910 sale : 15,000. Revised 1939. |
| Routledge & Kegan Paul | Routledge's Complete Letter Writer for Ladies and Gentlemen in Society, in Love and in Business | | 8,490 | No | |
| Secker & Warburg | The Park | Margaret Forster | 4,250 | Yes | Novel. Published May. |
| Staples Press | Cost of Economic Growth | E. J. Misham | 4,353 | No | 'Two Schwarz reviews helped.' |
| Studio Vista | Basic Design: Dynamic of Visual Form | Maurice Saunarez | 14,909 | No | First published 1964. |
| Souvenir Press | International Football Book No. 10 | | 22,274 | No | +20,000 Mail Order. |
| Souvenir Press | A Happier Sex Life | Dr Sha Kokken | 14,490 | No | Translated from Japanese. |
| Thames & Hudson | The Age of Expansion | Trevor-Roper (Ed.) | 7,117 | No | Published August. 6th in series. |
| University of London Press | English for Libya | | 230,000 | No | Government contract. |
| Weidenfeld & Nicolson | The Double Helix | Watson and Crick | 23,200 | Yes | DNA story. |

* Figures not available for Cape best-seller: The Naked Ape.   † Figures not available for Cassell Dictionaries.

# APPENDIX II

## A Selection of London Publishers

A comprehensive if dry list of British and Irish publishers is published annually in *The Writers' and Artists' Year Book*, and for enthusiasts Alex Hamilton has documented the financial and administrative details of the top twenty British publishers in *The Author*. (Spring and Summer, 1969). But the most satisfactory general guide to the London publishing scene is Cassell's *Directory of Publishing*.

What follows is a selection of publishers chosen for their size, significance and sometimes oddity – inclusion is on no other basis. First, Second and Third Eleven is perhaps a misnomer, as it doesn't describe the quality of the operation but the size of the team. London publishers are less free with up-to-date figures than their New York counterparts, so these categories are based on intelligent conjecture where no figures could be gleaned.

*W.H. ALLEN & CO., 43 Essex Street, Strand, London WC2
*Ownership*. Mark Goulden, when editor of *The Sunday Referee*, bought this ancient outfit for four thousand pounds before the war, sold it for many hundreds of thousands to Doubleday, bought it back, sold it to Walter Reade the American film-maker, who sold his interest to Howard and Wyndham, the theatre managing chain. . . . his stepson Jeffrey Simmons is the present chief executive, and is on the board of Howard and Wyndham.

* Throughout the Appendix the asterisk indicates that the house is independent, i.e. not substantially owned by a non-publishing commercial group or printing interest.

*Character.* Flashy American-originated best-sellers (Goulden spends more time than anybody in New York); *Saturday Night and Sunday Morning*; the range is from pop to Kitsch, queer Imperial Rome.

*Size.* Second Eleven.

*Authors.* Alan Sillitoe, Jacqueline Susann, Edmund Wilson.

* ALLEN & UNWIN LTD, Ruskin House, 40 Museum Street, London WC1

*Ownership.* For years, Sir Stanley Unwin was the doyen of the book trade and wrote a rival publication – *The Truth About Publishing* – a book which has been translated into every known language. He was a super-salesman for British books and figured in every controversy and on every committee. The ownership is mostly with the family.

*Character.* Illustrious, academic and institutional, but they published *Kon-Tiki*.

*Size.* Definitely First Eleven.

*Authors.* Julian Huxley, Bertrand Russell, J. R. R. Tolkien.

*ALLISON & BUSBY, 6a Noel Street, Soho, London W1

*Ownership.* Clive Allison and Margaret Busby (he white, she coloured) plus eighteen smarty-pants young city gentlemen each with a modest investment.

*Character.* The most brilliant new imprint in terms of fiction for a decade. *The Spook Who Sat By The Door* by Sam Greenlees would be a typical A. & B. They get a lot of publicity and they deserve it. Jack Trevor Story, a solid, intellectual British writer, has just signed to them on a long-term contract, saying that he wanted a personal association with a publisher, as opposed to the impersonal one authors experienced in a large house.

*Size.* Tiny as yet, but watch out.

*Authors.* As above.

* ARLINGTON BOOKS, 15 Duke Street, St. James's, London SW1

*Ownership.* Desmond Elliott (q.v.).

*Character.* Cheeky, daft, sentimental, small at £30,000 turnover, but profitable. Mostly non-fiction, e.g., *How to Detect Fake Antiques* (John Fitzmaurice Mills). Elliott also masterminds operations like *The Dolly Dolly Spy* (Adam Diment) and *The Virgin Soldiers* (Leslie Thomas) as an agent.

*Size.* Pint.

*Authors.* Peg Bracken (of *The I Hate to Cook Book*), etc.

ASSOCIATED BOOK PUBLISHERS LTD, often known as A.B.P.

*Ownership.* Public. An amalgam of traditional British firms, dominated by Methuen (publishers of *Winnie-the-Pooh*), and including Eyre & Spottiswoode, Chapman & Hall Ltd, Evelyn Waugh's publishers, now wholly scientific, and the extremely profitable legal firms of Sweet & Maxwell Ltd and Stevens & Sons Ltd.

*Character.* An immense output. Chairman – Sir Oliver Crosthwaite-Eyre, D.L. Profitable Commonwealth publishing interests all over plus a travel agency 'Eyre Travel'.

*Size.* First Eleven.

*Authors.* From Einstein to Jilly Cooper, including John Braine, J. P. Donleavy, Christopher Isherwood, Joy Packer, Mervyn Peake and top playwrights.

JOHN BAKER LTD, 5 Royal Opera Arcade, Pall Mall, London SW1

*Ownership.* John Baker bought it with the Unicorn Press and The Richards Press from Martin Secker, originally of Secker & Warburg, who himself had bought Grant Richards's inheritance which included some Housman, some Lawrence and *The Ragged Trousered Philanthropists*. Taken over by A. & C. Black.

*Character.* Exquisite 'nineties and Edwardian literature, beautifully printed.

*Size.* Minute, in a charming locale.

*Authors.* As above plus donnish belles-lettrists.

* A. & C. BLACK LTD, 4, 5 and 6 Soho Square, London W1
*Ownership*. Public company, but effective control in family/board
   hands. The current Black is a great-grandson of the founder
   (1807).
*Character*. The most famous reference publishers in England,
   viz. *Who's Who*.
*Size*. Second Eleven and extremely profitable. Turnover in 1970,
   with John Baker, £898,000

* BASIL BLACKWELL & MOTT LTD, 49 Broad Street, Oxford
*Ownership*. The Blackwell family.
*Character*. Apart from running the most impressive-looking book-
   shop in the kingdom (second, perhaps, to Heffer's in Cam-
   bridge), from their vantage point in the Broad they snap up a lot
   of dons and also have a school list. Rather stuffy. NB. Sir
   Basil was a witness against *Last Exit to Brooklyn*.
*Size*. Second Eleven. No undergraduates should imagine that
   their fiction will be looked at here.
*Authors*. Hugh Clegg, L. G. W. Fealey, J. M. Thompson.

ANTHONY BLOND LTD, 56 Doughty Street, London WC1
*Ownership*. Acquired 1969 by C.B.S., U.S.A., and managed by
   original owners Anthony Blond and Desmond Briggs, who
   went independent from C.B.S. in mid 1971 to start their own
   list from the same premises.
*Character*. Started in the late 'fifties with partly sexy, partly upper-
   class British fiction. Now sobered up and has possibly brightest
   post-war school book list under Blond Educational imprint.
*Size*. Verging on Second Eleven.
*Authors*. Gillian Freeman, Jean Genet, Simon Raven, Alan
   Williams.

* CALDER & BOYARS LTD, 18 Brewer Street, London W1
*Ownership*. John Calder and Marion Boyars.
*Character*. Continental, classy and uncompromisingly highbrow
   novels, poetry and plays. *The Tropic of Cancer* (Henry Miller)

swept all their losses away and their persistence over *Last Exit to Brooklyn* (Hubert Selby), which was acquitted of obscenity by Mr Justice Salmon, made John Calder the leader of the 'abolish censorship' movement in Britain. A chaotic office produces profits at just under a £100,000-a-year turnover.

*Size.* Second Eleven.

*Authors.* Beckett, Ionesco, Alexander Trocchi, Ferlinghetti, Robbe-Grillet.

---

\* JONATHAN CAPE LTD, 30 Bedford Square, London WC1

*Ownership.* Controlled by an equally balanced board of Cape and Chatto directors with the happy feature of joint chairmen – Ian Parsons of Chatto and Graham C. Greene of Cape. Despite an 18 per cent Granada interest, Cape (and Chatto too) belongs to the handful of remaining independent houses.

*Character.* Probably the busiest literary publisher in London. *Catch-22*, Philip Roth and John Lennon are coups of chairman Tom Maschler; associated companies are Cape Goliard Press, who publish poetry, and Jackdaw Publications.

*Size.* Because they have no basic educational turnover they are probably still in the Second Eleven financially, though First in almost anything else.

*Authors.* Ian Fleming, Ernest Hemingway, T. E. Lawrence, Arthur Ransome and top moderns.

---

\* CHATTO & WINDUS LTD, 40–42 William IV Street, London WC2

*Ownership.* Until recently one of the last surviving partnerships in London, now associated with Jonathan Cape (see above). Distinguished by having one of the few women publishers as managing director – Norah Smallwood. Chairman Ian Parsons.

*Character.* Elegant literature and criticism.

*Size.* Second Eleven.

*Authors.* Richard Hoggart, Aldous Huxley, Proust, Lytton

Strachey, Virginia Woolf (via her husband Leonard Woolf, of The Hogarth Press).

* WILLIAM COLLINS SONS & CO. LTD (q.v.), 14 St James's Place, London SW1

*Ownership.* Public Company with a heavy family stake.

*Character.* Dynamic seventy-year-old Billy Collins runs the hottest commercial enterprise in British publishing, selling eight million pounds worth of books per annum, with the most envied sales force in the publishing world. Strong on natural history and middle-brow best-sellers like Alistair MacLean, (80,000 copies average sales) under his Fontana imprint he has branched out into high-powered campus backs, 'Modern Masters'. Lady Collins works on the religious side.

*Size.* Top of the First Eleven.

*Authors.* Joy Adamson, Teilhard de Chardin, Agatha Christie, Hammond Innes, (averaging 60,000 copies per book), C. V. Wedgwood.

* LEO COOPER & SEELEY SERVICE LTD, 196 Shaftesbury Avenue, London WC2

*Ownership.* Leo Cooper and Tom Hartman joined up with Seeley Service, the publisher of the Lonsdale Library, a must for country gentlemen.

*Character.* Their list still bristles with military titles, but made a splash when they started, with *Accidental Agent* (John Goldsmith), a hair-raising, stiff-upper-lip secret-agent yarn.

*Size.* Modest.

*Authors.* Sui generis.

DAVID & CHARLES LTD, South Devon House, Railway Station, Newton Abbot, Devon

*Ownership.* Founded in the 'sixties and once a partnership; now Hambros has a large stake.

*Character.* Reprints of Bradshaw, books on railways and the nine-

teenth-century environment; cunning and charming advertising.
*Size.* Second Eleven.


ANDRÉ DEUTSCH LTD (q.v.), 105 Great Russell Street, London
WC1
*Ownership.* Original shareholders André Deutsch, Nicholas
Bentley and Diana Athill joined by a 40 per cent stake from
Time-Life.
*Character.* Hot political sensations from Philby to Krushchev, laced
with high-level fiction (Francis Wyndham rediscovered Jean
Rhys for them). Cookery, children's books and a specialist
library list are sound make-weights. George Mikes's *How to be
an Alien*, which André bought back from Allan Wingate, still
sells 5,000 a year at 80p.
*Size.* Second Eleven.
*Authors.* V. S. Naipaul, Terry Southern, *Sunday Times* Insight
Team, the Symposium on Public Lending Right, John Updike.


* DENNIS DOBSON, 80 Kensington Church Street, London W8.
*Ownership.* Dennis Dobson, Margaret Dobson.
*Character.* An enormous, slightly scatty list, with the occasional
flash of genius. Very much run out of a family house as a
family business. Bring in a lot of science fiction from America
and publish inventive children's books.
*Size.* Modest.
*Authors.* Gerard Hoffnung, Spike Milligan.


*FABER & FABER LTD, 3 Queen Square, London WC1.
*Ownership.* The Faber family and other directors.
*Character.* Was certainly the most distinguished literary imprint;
T. S. Eliot was a director. A wide list characterized by strong,
chic, letterpress jackets. A lot of monographs in the objects of
virtue fields, and books on manure.
*Size.* First Eleven.

*Authors*. Lawrence Durrell, T. S. Eliot, William Golding, Robert Lowell, Ezra Pound.

GARNSTONE PRESS, GEOFFREY BLES, 59 Brompton Road, London SW3.

*Ownership*. Coming up fast on the outside among London publishers is Michael Balfour; in his early thirties, Balfour started Garnstone Press with £3,000 in 1965.

*Character*. General non-fiction (his own annual guidebook *Help Yourself in London* is now famous). In April 1971 he shrewdly bought the forty-seven-year-old Geoffrey Bles imprint (publishers of C. S. Lewis's *The Screwtape Letters*) from Collins, and is maintaining its traditional list.

*Size:* Third Eleven.

★ VICTOR GOLLANCZ LTD, 14 Henrietta Street, Covent Garden, London WC2

*Ownership*. About fifty private shareholders, with the family in voting control.

*Character*. This product of the late 'twenties – the Left Book Club, Dorothy L. Sayers – still pumps out exciting thrillers, but the founder's death has left its mark.

*Size*. Second Eleven.

*Authors*. Ivy Compton Burnett, Lord George-Brown, Michael Innes, Daphne du Maurier, Ignazio Silone.

★ GUINNESS SUPERLATIVES LTD, 24 Upper Brook Street, London W1

*Ownership*. Arthur Guinness, Son & Co. Ltd. Norris and Ross McWhirter, twin brothers, are the compilers and editors.

*Character*. For years they published only one book, *The Guinness Book of Records*, and owned one printing press to print it; the profits are immaterial.

*Size*. Small, but non-fiction titles are added at the rate of six to eight a year.

HAMISH HAMILTON LTD, 90 Great Russell Street, London WC1
*Ownership.* The Thomson group.
*Character.* Founded in the 'thirties by 'Jamie' Hamilton, this firm rapidly became a smart London publisher, specializing in French literature and high-class books of American origin. Professor Sir Denis Brogan is a member of the board.
*Size.* Second Eleven.
*Authors.* Lord Butler, J. K. Galbraith, L. P. Hartley, Nancy Mitford, Alan Moorehead, Simenon.

WILLIAM HEINEMANN LTD, 15–16 Queen Street, London W1
*Ownership:* This Victorian firm, whose founder was a Jew, is now part of the Thomas Tilling original diversified empire.
*Character.* Still one of Britain's biggest publishers, rivalling A.B.P. and Collins. They have educational and medical subsidiaries, both of which are highly profitable, but are famous in the market-place for best-sellers and smart operations, mainly engineered by Charles Pick, once a traveller for Victor Gollancz.
*Size.* First Eleven.
*Authors.* D. H. Lawrence, Anthony Powell, J. B. Priestley, Somerset and all the Maughams.

\* HODDER & STOUGHTON LTD, St Paul's House, Warwick Lane, London EC4.
*Ownership.* The Hodder-Williams and Attenborough family.
*Character.* A never terribly distinguished, bourgeois British imprint, with yellow fiction predominant. It has been given a new look by Robin Denniston. The Hodder Group also publish the Teach Yourself series of which millions of copies are in print, and includes the Brockhampton Press, a profitable middlebrow children's fiction imprint.
*Size.* First Eleven.
*Authors.* John Buchan, R. F. Delderfield, Baroness Orczy, Anthony Sampson, Mary Stewart, and ex-Gollancz, ex-Heinemann, Le Carré.

I

HUTCHINSON PUBLISHING GROUP LTD, 178–202 Great Portland Street, London W1

*Ownership.* This huge, once wobbly amalgam is the inheritor of Mr (never quite Sir) Walter Hutchinson's printing activities and comprises a large number of fairly Third-Eleven publishing imprints, although under their main colophon, a classy bull conceived by Sir Robert Lusty himself, some high-powered titles are produced.

*Character.* Specializes in the occult, mystery, sport and so forth. This has recently been tidied up by Sir Robert Lusty and Noel Holland. They launched New Authors Ltd, which was designed as a profit-sharing first-novelists' operation but never quite got off the ground.

*Size.* First Eleven.

*Authors.* Svetlana Alliluyeva, Barbara Cartland, Maureen Duffy, Arthur Koestler, Dennis Wheatley.

MICHAEL JOSEPH LTD, 52 Bedford Square, London WC1

*Ownership.* The Thomson group.

*Character.* It used to be the most efficient purveyor of middle-class, middlebrow fiction, e.g. Monica Dickens,★ Richard Gordon,★ in Britain. Michael Joseph the founder was once married to to Hermione Gingold and loved cats.

*Size.* Second Eleven.

*Authors.* James Baldwin, Paul Gallico, John and Anthony Masters, 'Miss Read'.

LONGMAN GROUP LTD, 74 Grosvenor Street, London W1

*Ownership.* With Penguin, part of the Cowdray organization.

*Character.* The oldest (1724) and one of the biggest publishers in London. Their turnover is mainly (about 95 per cent) from educational books, but their general trade list is distinguished and respectable. Immensely strong overseas. For a long time shared with O.U.P. and Nelson's the fruits from Africa's dry

★ Moved to Heinemann, following Charles Pick.

soil. They are still far the biggest publishers in, for instance, Rhodesia.

*Size*. Top of the First Eleven.

*Authors*. Francis King, Gavin Maxwell, Mary Renault, Wilfred Thesiger.

★ MACMILLAN & CO. LTD, 4 Little Essex Street, London WC2

*Ownership*. The Macmillans.

*Character*. Not quite so anciently established but rivals to Longman's in almost every textbook field, which is about 60 per cent of their business. Famous for both classy and best-selling fiction.

*Size*. First Eleven.

*Authors*. Jane Duncan, Eric Linklater, C. P. Snow, Muriel Spark, John Wain, Rebecca West.

★ MILLS & BOON LTD, 50 Grafton Way, Fitzroy Square, London W1

*Ownership*. The Boon family.

*Character*. Almost the only imprint in London that has given its name to a type of book. Once, in library fiction, old ladies would ask for another three Mills & Boons. Suddenly successful in paperbacking their own pulp fiction, and also bright and inventive in the secondary modern educational field. John Boon is a pillar of the book trade.

*Size*. Second Eleven, but coming up to £1 million turnover p.a.

*Authors*. Irrelevant.

★ JOHN MURRAY LTD, 50 Albemarle Street, London W1

*Ownership*. Since the eighteenth century there has always been someone called John Murray looking after John Murray.

*Character*. As above, with a grand little list of English authors, notably Sir John Betjeman, Kenneth Clark. Publishers of Byron and the early Disraeli. Their school list includes the best secondary science textbooks.

*Size*. Second Eleven.

*Authors*. John Betjeman, Lesley Blanch, Kenneth Clark.

\* PETER OWEN LTD, 12 Kendrick Mews. Kendrick Place, London SW7

*Ownership*. Peter Owen (managing) and Wendy F. Owen.

*Character*. A small, post-war, eccentric publisher with a tendency to do remote Rumanian poets.

*Size*. Third Eleven.

*Authors*. Blaise Cendrars, Herman Hesse, Violette Leduc.


\* OXFORD UNIVERSITY PRESS (q.v.), Ely House, 37 Dover Street, London W1

*Ownership*. Oxford University, via gentlemen called the Delegates.

*Character*. The largest academic press in the world, with twenty-one branches in, among other places, America, Canada and India. Stately, well-bred, but a deal more aggressive than their Cambridge counterparts. Apart from a polymath scholarly list they have a neat line in children's books.

*Size*. Discreet about figures, they are probably the biggest publishers in England, in titles if not in turnover (but see note p. 17).

*Authors*. Top sinologists, psephologists, epistemologists – you name it.


GEORGE RAINBIRD LTD, Marble Arch House, 44 Edgware Road, London W2

*Ownership*. Thomson Organization.

*Character*. Pioneer of the packaged book, viz. *The Sun King*. George Rainbird, once an employee of Wolf Foges, understood the art of international publishing early on. He doesn't initiate much under his own imprint but will undertake to sell an edition to publishers at a *prix-fixe*. Extremely successful in this non-bookish, faintly art field, e.g. Wilfred Blunt's *The Dream King*.


MARTIN SECKER & WARBURG LTD, 14 Carlisle Street, London W1

*Ownership*. Heinemann, q.v. (i.e. Tilling).

*Character*. Revolves around the character of Fred Warburg, author of a book on publishing called *An Occupation for Gentlemen*. Specializes in classy European fiction and the occasional Japanese adventure. But watch out for Tom Rosenthal (q.v.).
*Size*. Modest.
*Authors*. Gunter Grass, Robert Musil, Italo Svevo, formerly Brigid Brophy.

SIDGWICK & JACKSON LTD, I Tavistock Chambers, Bloomsbury Way, London WC1
*Ownership*. Substantially Charles Forte, whom the original owner, Jim Knapp-Fisher, knew as a head-waiter before the war. The Longford family have moved in.
*Character*. An energetic putsch is being launched to enliven this imprint.
*Size*. Changing every day.
*Authors*. Antonia Fraser (Lord Longford's daughter), Patrick Moore, Cecil King, Flook.

* CHARLES SKILTON LTD, 50 Alexandra Road, Wimbledon SW19
*Ownership*. Owner-driven.
*Character*. Elegant erotica and de luxe editions. Mr Skilton is a leading light in the Independent Publishers Guild, who are supplementary in a sense to the Publishers' Association (q.v.).
*Size*. Modest.

* SOUVENIR PRESS LTD, 95 Mortimer Street, London W1
*Ownership*. Ernest Hecht, whose two chief passions are bull-fighting and football.
*Character*. Popular, with-it, not so elegantly produced but consistently successful small general list. Probably the most profitable private publisher in London, famous for unexpected hits like *Chariots of the Gods* (Daniken) and *Trachtenberg's Speed System of Mathematics* (Trachtenberg). Co-publisher with Michael Joseph of *Airport* (Arthur Hailey).

*Size*. Second Eleven.

*Authors*. This inventive house depends on ideas rather than authors.

\* NEVILLE SPEARMAN LTD, 112 Whitfield Street, London W1
*Ownership*. Mr and Mrs Neville Armstrong.

*Character*. Much a reflection of the above. Plucky, adventurous fiction and splashy non-fiction like *The ABC of Love*. Mr Armstrong once lured a recalcitrant author to his house and locked him in until he'd finished a book.

*Size*. Modest.

*Authors*. Original publishers of J. P. Donleavy's *The Ginger Man*.

\* THAMES & HUDSON LTD, 30–34 Bloomsbury Street, London WC1
*Ownership*. The Neurath family.

*Character*. This post-war firm really invented, as far as England is concerned, international art editions, stealing some of Phaidon's clothes in the process. They branched out under the guidance of the erudite Third Programme editor, Tom Rosenthal, who has now moved to Secker & Warburg, into documentary non-fiction.

*Size*. Probably First Eleven, certainly very profitable.

*Authors*. Asa Briggs, Joan Evans, Alan Watts (Zen expert).

\* MAURICE TEMPLE SMITH LTD, 37 Great Russell Street, London WC1
*Ownership*. Mr & Mrs Temple Smith, plus Tata of London, a subsidiary of the Indian industrial monolith.

*Character*. Dependent on the owner/driver who made his name with John Braine's *Room at the Top* (rejected by many others) while an editor at Eyre & Spottiswoode, moved to Secker & Warburg where he became managing director, had a difference of opinion with Fred Warburg (q.v.) and set up on his own. Historical and topical non-fiction. Twenty titles a year. (N.B. Believes fiction publishing will become a speciality for a few publishers only).

*Size.* Third Eleven.
*Authors.* Martin Esslin.

WARD, LOCK & CO. LTD, 116 Baker Street, London W1
*Ownership.* Formerly the Lock and Shipton family, as of 1971,
a property company.
*Character.* Publishers of Mrs Beeton's Cook Books and romantic
fiction à la Mills & Boon, plus children's books.
*Size.* Second Eleven.
*Authors.* The late Mrs Beeton, Dornford Yates.

GEORGE WEIDENFELD & NICOLSON LTD, 5 Winsley
Street, Oxford Circus, London W1
*Ownership.* George Weidenfeld and Encyclopaedia Britannica
with a big minority share (Senator Benton of the U.S.A.).
*Character.* Self-proliferating intelligentsia, international series plus
high social speed. Party-giving Sir George Weidenfeld is
married to a rich American lady and has made a thumping
controversial impact on the London publishing scene since the
war. Employs Tony Godwin at eight thousand a year.
*Size.* Second Eleven.
*Authors.* Saul Bellow, Abba Eban, Antonia Fraser, Norman
Mailer, Nabokov.

★ WOLFE PUBLISHING LTD, 10 Earlham Street, London WC2
*Ownership.* Peter Wolfe, one of André Deutsch's many ex-sales-
managers.
*Character.* An extension of the greetings-card business in book
form. An immensely successful international operation,★ with
best-sellers, like *The Good Loo Guide.*
*Size.* Coming up on the outside, with £500,000-worth of sales
promotional books.
*Authors.* Jonathan Routh.

★ Wolfe also distributes the books of Reg Davis-Poynter, the latest of those who
believe in publishing as a 'cottage industry with connections to the mains'.

# APPENDIX III

## The Literary Agents

This honourable profession is asked to excuse the errors and omissions in the following eclectic but, it is hoped, not prejudiced list of literary agents. It is designed to help aspiring authors and publishers to find their way around a sensitive but crucial area in both their lives. Since personality is more important than substance in the agency world, the new top people are fairly volatile and this list will have to be checked against the bland but comprehensive list in *The Writers' and Artists' Year Book* or in Cassell's *Directory of Publishing*.

Finally, this is a list of agents who sell books to publishers, not plays or film scripts or television scripts, so although, say, Margaret Ramsay could be the best play agent in London, she will not appear here:

CURTIS BROWN LTD, 13 King Street, Covent Garden, London WC2.

One of the oldest, biggest and best equipped literary agents in London with seventy employees and all kinds of specialists. The older authors are handled by Graham Watson and Juliet O'Hea, others by Richard Simon. Their clients include Sir John Betjeman, Penelope Gilliatt, John Wain, Christopher Isherwood, Gore Vidal, Al Alvarez, and Colin Spencer.

ROSICA COLIN, 4 Hereford Square, London, SW7.

Represents Beckett, Ionesco and Genet, a very subtle sort of hat trick. Also a lot of London publishers for Continental rights.

DIANA CRAWFURD, 5 King Street, Covent Garden, London WC2.

This beautiful country gel is a relative newcomer but no slouch. She represents the literary output of Mr David Frost and Messrs Rennie Airth, Christopher Booker, Anthony Jay and James Pope Hennessy.

TOBY EADY LTD, 27 Chesham Place, London, SW1

Very much a new luminary. Represents Alistair Hamilton, Ted Lewis, David Spanier, Michael Storey and a number of authors who, they claim, will be well known in a few years time.

JOHN FARQUHARSON LTD, 15 Red Lion Square, London WC1.

Here Innes Rose and George Greenfield operate an old-fashioned agency which specializes in sporting and adventurous figures, e.g. Lord George-Brown, in the first category and Sir Francis Chichester, Sir Edmund Hillary, Sir Vivian Fuchs and Pat Smythe, in the second.

A. M. HEATH & CO. LTD, 35 Dover Street, London W1.

Another dependable if soft-hitting agency started after the First World War, now run by Mark Hamilton and Michael Thomas. A number of American books through their associates, Brandt & Brandt Inc.

PETER JANSON-SMITH LTD, 42 Great Russell Street, London WC1.

Peter Janson-Smith used to run the foreign rights department of Curtis Brown and is therefore a specialist in this area. He is the only literary agent to be on the Royal Literary Fund and is active in publishing politics. He represents Eric Ambler, the estate of Ian Fleming, Professor Parkinson and Alan Williams amongst many others. Also at his office, once the home of the late-lamented Putnam's, he shelters Elaine Greene, John Wolfers (q.v.) and Murray Pollinger, who run their separate agencies. They once employed Deborah Rogers (q.v.), who split to start her own operation.

HOPE LERESCHE & STEELE, 11 Jubilee Place, Chelsea, London SW3.

A successor to the estate of J. B. Pinker, probably the founder of all literary agencies (he represented H. G. Wells). Hope Leresche handles the Liverpool poet Roger McGough and a number of Americans like James Jones, Irwin Shaw and William Styron, plus the controversial Swiss playwright, Friedrich Dürrenmatt.

A. D. PETERS AND CO., 10 Buckingham Street, Adelphi, London WC2.

They inhabit a tiny palazzo off the Strand and boast a dining-room. Michael Sissons is possibly the most brilliantly belligerent agent in London, and clients of this firm rattle with laurels. Mr Peters's own authors include Arthur Koestler, Rebecca West, V. S. Pritchett, J. B. Priestley, Sir Julian Huxley, and this firm handles both Mortimers, Professor Hugh Trevor-Roper, Anthony Sampson, and, among the younger ones, David Pryce-Jones, Isabel Colegate and Auberon Waugh.

LAURENCE POLLINGER LTD, 18 Maddox Street, London W1.

This is a big shop and was bigger when united with Higham under the title of Pearn, Pollinger and Higham (known some-times as Pee, Pie, Po). Much of their revenue must come from the estates of the literary departed like D. H. Lawrence, Scott Fitzgerald and Grantly Dick-Read. Their current clients include H. E. Bates, Graham Greene and Alan Moorehead. They also represent (too?) many U.S. publishers. A baby Pollinger, Murray (q.v.), recently quit the nest to shelter under Peter Janson-Smith's umbrella.

DEBORAH ROGERS, 29 Goodge Street, London W1.

A bright, pretty girl who is advancing steadily with clients like Anthony Burgess and Mordecai Richler, she will be helped by her connections with Candida Donadio, the New York agent whose clients she represents, and with Lynn Nesbit in New York. She also handles Cyril Connolly and S. J. Perelman.

A. P. WATT & SON, 26–8 Bedford Row, London WC1.

Started in 1875. Claim to be the oldest literary agency. They still make money out of writers like Rider Haggard, Kipling, Baroness Orczy, Rafael Sabatini, Wells, and Yeats. More recently they have handled the affairs of Brian Aldiss, Michael Holroyd and Svetlana Alliluyeva. The two principals are Michael Horniman and Hilary Rubinstein, a nephew of the late Sir Victor Gollancz.

JOHN WOLFERS, 42 Great Russell Street, London WC1.

A typical adventurous packaging newcomer of an agent who points out that he is too young (in business) to represent dead authors. He specializes in satisfying the middlebrow non-fiction market, with an eye on the *Sunday Times* serial. His clients tend to be popularizing academics and high-powered journalists like the Calders (Ritchie and Nigel) and the Cockburns (James and Alexander).

Note

It is typical of the volatility of the world of literary agents that two of Watt's clients also appear on other agents' lists. It also points to the infinite divisibility of copyright in that authors sometimes divide their creative activity between different agents. Any inaccuracies in this list must be forgiven therefore, and of course the names of their 'clients', as they call them, are typical and not comprehensive.

---

# A Glossary of Terms used in Publishing

NOTE: Publishers have a jargon like every other profession, much of it drawn from the print world but some of it their own. Here are some frequently used words and expressions.

*Advance* Sum paid by publishers to authors before publication on account of royalties which it is hoped will be earned.

*Art paper* (*U.S. coated paper*) Glossy paper suitable for the reproduction of illustrations in a book.

*B.A.* Booksellers' Association.

*Best-seller* No strict usage. For a brief discussion see pp. 55-7 and Appendix I.

*Blurb* Publishers' description of a book, printed on the jacket flap, designed to appeal to reviewers, booksellers and the public.

*Block* (*U.S. engravings*) Mechanically or chemically engraved metal plate used in the letterpress process for reproducing line or halftone illustrations.

*Bulk* Technically the width of the book without the binding, but often used as a transitive verb meaning to bulk out a thin book by using heavier paper and make it appear more substantial than the text alone allows.

*Cadet Edition* The rude words taken out for children, e.g. *The Cruel Sea*.

*Colophon* A publisher's symbol, originally printed on the last page, now usually on the title page.

*Copyright* © *1971* The exclusive right of an author to produce his own work and protection against plagiarism of every signatory of the Berne Convention (1956).

*Direct* A MS which comes direct from an author, as opposed to through an agent, and can be contracted 'direct'.

*Direct mail* To supply customers in this way upsets the B.A. (q.v.).

*Edition* A version of a book, first, second, revised, unexpurgated, or whatever, often confused with 'impression' (q.v.).

*Editor* The man or woman in a publishing office who deals with the author and his work. (The French for publisher is *éditeur*, which is confusing.)

*Endpapers* The two blank fly leaves at the beginning and end of a book, pasted to the boards. Sometimes these are decorated, or are printed with maps, genealogical tables, etc.

*Figures* A publisher will say 'two and a half', 'five' or even 'fifty', meaning thousands of copies or pounds, e.g. 'We had to print seven (thousand copies) because we paid two and a half (thousand pounds) for it.'

*Folio* The page number.

*General (U.S. 'Trade') Publishing* Any publishing which is not specialist, educational or technical.

*Hardback* A book which is bound in boards and cloth, as opposed to a paperback or 'soft back'.

*Impression* All the copies of a book printed at one time from the same type or plates. There can be many impressions of one edition (q.v.).

*Imprint* The publisher's name.

*(I)SBN* (International) Standard Book Number. Every book has this code which shows the imprint—the first three digits—and title—the following six digits; of a book; a British invention intended to become international, and so be of use in ordering books.

*Letterpress* Printing from raised characters – the oldest method of printing.

*Litho(graphy)* Printing from smooth plate or cylinder.

*Machine (v.t.)* The action of printing by letterpress or by lithography.

*Net* The price of a book in a bookshop is a net price below which the bookseller may not sell without permission. This apparent breach of Retail Price Maintenance has been supported by the Restrictive Practices Court.

*Non-book* Scornful description of a publication designed to appeal to those who regard a book as an object to look at rather than to read.

*Non-net* Technically the opposite of net. In fact applies only to books sold to institutions like schools through educational contractors. The whole structure of discounts between net and non-net is different (see Chapter 8).

*One-off* A 'one-off' author or a 'one-off' book means that the publisher thinks the author has only one book in him, or that he has borrowed an author from another publisher for a specific series.

*Outright* Articles for symposia, or even whole books, can be bought outright by a publisher, i.e. with no royalty payments.

*P.A.* Publishers' Association.

*'Perfect' binding* A method of binding a book with hot glue on to guillotined sheets, i.e. no sewing.

*Perfect number* or even working – when a book can be printed and bound in sections of 32 pages – i.e. most economically.

*Permissions* Fees payable by publishers wishing to reprint passages in excess of 300 words from another author (fewer words for verse). Music is particularly expensive and tricky.

*Prelims* The pages before the main text of a book, often given roman numerals.

*Public domain* Anything in print fifty years after the author's death, or after posthumous first publication, is not in copyright.

*Pulp (v.t.)* Books, usually paperbacks, which it is impossible to remainder or dump, are 'pulped' and new paper made of them.

*'Pulp' fiction* Cheap novels.

*River of white* Accidental optical effect caused by vertical juxtaposition of spaces between lines.

*Royalties* Percentage of the *published* price of a book payable to the author.

*Setting* Sometimes called composing. The act of a printer who transcribes a typescript on to a machine.

*Sheet deal* Sale of flat or folded and collated (assembled) sheets of an edition to another (U.S.) publisher or library contractor.

*Sight unseen* A purchase of a book thought to be of such value and urgency that the publisher has to put down money without seeing the MS.

*Softcover or paperback* A book printed on a rotary machine, with a soft paper cover.

*Subscription* The number of copies ordered by booksellers prior to publication.

*Wash top (U.S. 'stained')* Colouring the top of a book to make it look prettier.

*Widow* Single word at the end top or bottom of a page. e.g. widow.

# APPENDIX V

## How to Get a Job in Publishing

1. Even Second Eleven publishers get two or three letters a day asking for jobs, mostly from about-to-be graduates. Think what the others are saying and try to produce a different sort of letter. (A sample appears below).

2. Type it. If you do get offered a job you won't have a secretary.

3. Subscribe to the *Bookseller*, concentrating on the ads, and *Smith's Trade News;* read Whitefriars, *the* gossip columnist.

4. Try and get a job in the vacation in a book shop. They usually need help over Christmas. Better still, work, even as a packer (*pace* the unions), for a publisher.

5. Write to as many publishers as you can think of. Apart from *The Writers' and Artists' Year Book*, the best guide is from the imprints on the titles which intrigue you in a public library or bookshop.

6. Before going to see any publisher, familiarize yourself with his titles, which you can do by asking for his catalogue. He won't know you've done this when he interviews you, and, publishers being vain, will be overwhelmed if you refer to an abstruse title he has published.

7. Don't be sniffy about where you go. Get in anywhere doing anything. You're more likely to get your first job from one of the big firms who run training schemes. That might mean living in Harlow (Longman's) or Basingstoke (Macmillan's) or Glasgow

(Collins's) for a few months. At your interview you may confess a weakness but not a passion for novels. Your ideas should be in the direction of non-fiction, education and even technical books.

8. If you are writing a novel yourself, keep quiet about it. Much better to imply that you have a number of friends far more brilliant than yourself who are hard at work and whom you could steer the publisher's way.

9. If you are just reading this book in a book shop, buy it.

## SAMPLE LETTER

This applicant wants an editorial job in the trade or general department and, of course, he has to show a lively mind and be intriguing. There are many other jobs in publishing, on the sales, production, publicity or technical sides, in which an applicant would be wiser to compose a more circumspect and factual missive.

170 *Finborough Road, London, SW*10.

Dear Mr Rosencrantz,

I would like to come and work for you.

Publishing as a career has interested me to the exclusion of anything else, and in the holidays from school and university[1] I have always been lucky enough to get part-time work in a book-shop – at first voluntary. Last summer I ran the Theology Department of Foyle's.[2]

Rosencrantz & Guildenstern's list seems to me an exciting combination of business acumen and literary experiment[3] and I am sure you've got a winner in *Bingo Stops for Ramadan*.[4]

I realize that book editing can be a complicated and laborious business but I've had some experience with juvenile magazines and I do know a lot of young people[5] who could be made to harness their talents for the eventual[6] benefit of R. & G.

Some quite decent people will vouch for my character.[7]

Yours sincerely,

JEREMY PADGETT*

* My apologies to the real Jeremy Padgetts (who wouldn't think of wanting a job in publishing), and my thanks for the use of their euphonious name.

K

1. He'd be careful not to list his 'O' and 'A' levels and honours, it is enough to throw away the fact that he has a degree; this reticence should intrigue. Further, there is no need to give his age as he is obviously in his early twenties.

2. This is not so unlikely as it looks. Foyle's have a large turnover in assistants as well as in books.

3. This is probably a mistake. Experiment in publishing equals, nearly always, total loss; in this context the word 'adventure' would be safer.

4. He's certainly been reading the *Bookseller* where R. & G. have been advertising this hopeful title.

5. Publishers always feel they *should* be in touch with younger people and the pain of being flooded out by junkie autobiographies is counteracted by Padgett's use of the word people.

6. 'eventual', which indicates that a lot of hard work will have to be done on these promising manuscripts before they are publishable.

7. This sentence is the property of Mr Edward Mace, who used it to obtain a job on the *Observer*.

Most applicants for jobs in publishing are, sadly, refused. We have devised the following form letter to reply to those who write to us.

Dear——

## WE'D LIKE TO HAVE YOU ON BOARD, BUT . . .

Thank you for your letter about wanting to work here. We are obviously touched that you should think of us, and the horrid reason for replying in this form is that you are not alone.

This small publishing firm, which employs about 23 people in the London Office, receives about a dozen letters a week from people who want jobs and, rather than reply shortly to each application, it has been thought more practical to reply at some length to everybody, giving the reasons why we must say no.

At the end of last year the British Printing Corporation decided virtually to disband their book publishing operation; this has resulted in the departure of 90 personnel, some highly trained and some with long service in publishing. This fact is not put in in a critical spirit but simply to state the economic situation in trade or general publishing has led to business men cutting down operations. It has meant that, for every editor working, there are two or three who would like his or her job.

So, until times change it is not exaggerating to regard general publishing overall, with a few glorious exceptionally continuously successful houses, as a depressed industry.

A lot of people find the idea of working in publishing attractive. They particularly see themselves – and why not – as editors of fiction and non-fiction. This is possibly the most difficult, because it is the most desirable, occupation to find. If you have any aptitude in the educational world especially in maths or science, you will find it much more easy to get a job, than if you are an arts graduate from the Universities with a general interest in general matters.

This doesn't mean to say that somebody with determination and talent, and the knowledge of where to apply when, cannot still get employment. It would help if you had had some stint in bookshops and were aware of the kind of titles which sell and the kind (most) which do not. It would also help if your interest lay in selling because it is probably easier to get a job as a sales representative on either the general or textbook sides, than go straight into the office. Alternatively, if you had some knowledge of book production and were prepared to start there, you might find more vacancies than in editorial departments.

Further, it is much more likely that large organizations, like Collins, who have an excellent training scheme, or the Oxford University Press who employ so many people, can find you a job than small publishers like ourselves.

I am sorry to have to write in this tone, in this way and can only hope you have better luck elsewhere.

Yours sincerely,

ANTHONY BLOND

# Bibliography

There is no shortage of books about books and any firm of publishers with a centenary will oblige with a largely self-congratulatory volume recording its achievements.

So, we have the *House of Longman, Dent, Macmillan, Collins, Blackwood*, best obtained from the publisher concerned.

*A Brief History of Cambridge University Press* is recommended. It is free.

Also recommended are: *An Occupation for Gentlemen* by Fred Warburg (Hutchinsons, London, 1959), *The Penguin Story* by Sir William Williams (Penguin, Harmondsworth, 1956) and, for a good idea of American publishing, *Publishers on Publishing*, edited by G. Gross (Secker & Warburg, London, 1962).

Sir Stanley Unwin's *The Truth about Publishing*, 7th edition (Allen & Unwin, London, 1960), remains the classic but, of course, does not relate the upheavals of the last decade. More recently, Michael Howard has written *Jonathan Cape, Publisher* (Cape, London, 1970), and Eric Hiscock a gossipy, fringy account of his relations with publishers and best-sellers called *The Last Boat to Folly Bridge* (Cassell's, London, 1970).

The best fictional portraits of publishers, both mentioned in this book, are in Samuel Butler's *The Way of all Flesh* and Fr. Rolfe on Grant Richards in his *Nicholas Crabbe* (Faber, London, 1960).

The best text on book-selling is *The Truth About Book Selling* by Thomas Joy (Pitman, London, 1955). He is a former President of the Booksellers' Association, but a remarkably progressive man, and runs Hatchard's, Piccadilly.

Finally, I would like to acknowledge G. Hepburn's *The Author's Empty Purse* (Oxford University Press, 1969), which is a witty and delightful history of literary agency.

For advice on careers in bookselling there is a booklet by John Hyams with just that title published by the Booksellers' Association, 152 Buckingham Palace Road, London SW1. The Charter Group of Booksellers at the same address, of whom too little has been said in this book, have a neat line in explanatory texts and figures, notably *Training for Bookselling*.

# INDEX